PREFACE

BIRTHDAYS ARE OCCASIONS FOR CELEBRATING THE present, reminiscing about the past, and casting tentative glances toward the future. This is no less true for institutions and events than it is for persons. In the tense ecclesiastical atmosphere of the tenth year of Pope Francis's pontificate, it was not to be imagined that the sixtieth birthday of the Second Vatican Council—begun on October 11, 1962, and itself a matter of controversy from the start— would pass by without many commemorative articles. And so it happened.

The last of the Catholic Church's twenty-one ecumenical councils would not be nearly so interesting to us today if it were no more than a meeting of bishops or a collection of documents. In reality, Vatican II is and will always be a *symbol*. For some, it was and continues to be a harbinger of revolutionary change, an overdue updating of an archaic religious body, an embrace of long-resisted modernity. Others take it as comforting proof of how the Holy Spirit leads the Church in every age to read the "signs of the times" and, in their light, to reformulate her teaching and reshape her pastoral strategies in ways more beneficial to modern Christians. For still others, the Council—both in its official direction and in how it was immediately implemented by authorities who claimed to speak on its behalf—muddied the clarity of Catholic doctrine, fomented an iconoclastic campaign against tradition, and welcomed worldliness in the name of outreach. Using inadequate labels, we might call these points of view progressive, conservative, and traditionalist.

This anthology includes many and varied examples of the conservative and traditionalist perspectives, because that is where a lively and important debate is taking place between those who blame the Council for the crisis and devastation we have witnessed in the Catholic Church in the West over the past sixty years and those who blame exclusively the subsequent "implementation" of the Council by a host of incompetent or manipulative agents.

As most of the articles herein were published very close to each other in time, I have organized the book alphabetically by author. This arrangement has the drawback of placing George Weigel's two essays at the end, despite the fact that they are frequently discussed by other contributors. The reader might therefore consider starting with Weigel and then proceeding to the rest.

May this collection help its readers to think well about momentous questions connected with the historical reality and reception of the Second Vatican Council, thus achieving a better grasp of what place it should have—or, as it may turn out, should not have—in the life of the Church.

PETER A. KWASNIEWSKI
Feast of Christ the King
October 30, 2022

Ecclesial Center-Right and Center-Left Strategies*

FR CLAUDE BARTHE

Res Novae
October 1, 2022

"VATICAN II, WE NEED MORE VATICAN II!" BUT THE reforming elixir has long since grown stale…

Reforming *what*, by the way? Francis's grand design, symbolized by *Prædicate Evangelium*, the constitution that reforms the Curia, is as much a reform of the Church according to the spirit of Vatican II as it is a reform of the Curia. There is certainly an ambiguity about the object—the Curia, the Church—which is prolonged and increased by the media, but the links between the two reforms are no less intrinsic: the reorganization of the Roman government necessarily has consequences for that of the whole Church.

This was clearly seen in the discussions that took place during the consistory at the end of August, when a sort of second and more solemn promulgation of the Constitution *Prædicate Evangelium* of March 19, 2022 was staged. It was presented to the College of Cardinals, which was given the floor—duly framed—to express its approval.

There were, however, some critics who underlined the ecclesial stakes of any reform of the central administration. Some cardinals raised the difficulty of appointing simple lay heads of dicasteries. Their request, invoking *Lumen Gentium* and the sacramentality of the episcopate, was rather vague. To summarize the real problem: a number of the prefects of the Curia have real powers of jurisdiction,

---

* Original title: "Pour une vraie réforme de l'Église." Translated by Peter Kwasniewski; published at *Rorate Caeli* on October 7, 2022.

especially to judge bishops and clerics, as well as to issue texts, responses, and sentences of doctrinal significance. They do receive this jurisdiction by delegation from the Pope, but they must have an intrinsic capacity to be granted it for these types of acts (judging, teaching), which derives from their quality as clerics. The abuse of the term "synodality" was also noted, as a kind of slogan that seeks to express an extension, to the entire "People of God," of the episcopal collegiality so dear to Vatican II. However, historically, as an Eastern cardinal pointed out, the word "synodality" is almost the equivalent of episcopal collegiality, because it refers precisely to a certain collegial exercise of episcopal power in the Eastern Churches. It is therefore not a suitable term for signifying a kind of democratization, which should rather be called "communiality."

Successive reforms in the line of Vatican II on an exhausted and divided Church

One must keep in mind that Vatican II, in four years, from 1962 to 1965, had overturned an edifice that was not only Tridentine, as is often said, but even Gregorian (from the Gregorian Reform in the eleventh century). In spite of all the crises, the Great Schism, the Protestant Reformation, the Revolution, and in a pathetic way in more recent times, the Church has continued to claim fully, as she did with great force during the "Gregorian moment," the principle of her freedom: Spouse of Christ, she has always been conscious of being the supernatural totality of his Mystical Body on earth.

However, Vatican II broke down this total plenitude that the Church claimed to be: by issuing a certain number of "intuitions" (religious freedom, ecumenism, principles of interreligious dialogue), this Council recognized the existence outside the Church of supernatural entities, admittedly incomplete; of salvific means, albeit deficient; of a communion with Christ, albeit imperfect.

As a result, magisterial texts in the vein of the encyclical *Quas Primas* on the institutional kingship of Christ have become obsolete. This "opening to the modern world" of ecclesiastical society, very concretely to liberal democracy, has been realized at the same time as a surge in the secularization of this world (unless indeed the ecclesiological reversal itself strongly contributed to an increase in this secularization), a phenomenon before which the men of the Church have been caught short. They had advanced a hundred steps, while the world had covered ten thousand. And the renewal appeared to have been a suicide: of all the political, spiritual, and disciplinary consequences that resulted, the most striking was the exhaustion of mission, the *raison d'être* of the Church of Christ, which could be seen in the rarefaction of the principal workers in the harvest, clerics and religious, and in the decreasing number of converts and practicing members.

Worse still, the body was not only crumbling, but was breaking apart. It soon became clear that the Council had not succeeded in uniting all around its project: the opposition of the conciliar minority, which had become the traditionalist opposition, energized by its liturgical dimension, proved impossible to eliminate, an opposition whose ranks have swelled especially under the present pontificate—a whole reformist or "restorationist" world which, in the end and whatever it may say, has never fully agreed with Vatican II. The unity of what remained of Catholicism has been shattered.

It is therefore in this context of a Church in the process of exhaustion and ever more divided that the reform of its central government was attempted, in connection with a global conception of what the reform of the whole Church should be, or, in other words, in connection with an understanding of Vatican II.

The first time, in order to respond to the Council's wishes, Paul VI, with the constitution *Regimini Ecclesiæ Universæ* of August 15, 1967, had profoundly reshaped the face of the Roman Curia, creating, among other things, new organisms (Councils for the Laity, for Christian Unity, etc.). The most emblematic change he made was the transformation of the Supreme Congregation of the Holy Office, which was responsible for the papal regulation of Catholic doctrine and which had no Prefect (the Pope reserving the right to direct it himself) into a Congregation for the Doctrine of the Faith.

John Paul II's Constitution *Pastor Bonus* of June 28, 1988, which mainly brought the functioning of the Curia into line with the new Code of Canon Law, did not make any fundamental changes. The real novelty of this curial reform was not in structures but in the replenishment of the governing personnel, which came—as was the case for the personnel connected with liturgical reform—from the conciliar majority. As appointments were made, Congregations and Councils became more or less progressive or became more or less conservative again.

Today, *Prædicate Evangelium* is meant to be a further implementation of the "spirit of the Council" in Roman government, as well as a model to be followed at all levels to promote a truly "conciliar reform" of the whole Church. One of the key changes is the demotion of the Dicastery of the Doctrine of the Faith to second place, behind that of Evangelization. But here again, the Curia is mainly new because its personnel has been "brought up to Bergoglian standards." As for the project of making a decisive qualitative conciliar leap for both the Curia and the Church as a whole, the anemia of the ecclesiastical body and the ever-increasing tensions that run through it make that seem like wishful thinking.

Attempts to restore lost unity: a double failure

When the Church approached the shores of the twenty-first century, the fundamental failure of Vatican II could be measured from the point of view that is primary for her, that of mission. Not only did she no longer convert, but the number of her faithful, her religious, and her priests was reduced to such an extent that she seemed to be on the verge of extinction, at least in the West. Vatican II, whose whole ambition had been to adapt the message to the sensibility of the men of this time and to attract them to a rejuvenated, transformed, modernized Church, did not even manage to interest them.

And above all, the passage of time has shown that a split, one might say a latent schism, occurred after Vatican II, dividing the Church between two currents, both composite but clearly identifiable: the first, for whom the Council had to be revisited or at least contained in its boundaries; the other, for whom it was merely a starting point for extrapolation. The project of reestablishing unity around this Council, which did not claim to be exercising an infallible magisterium—in other words, which was not a principle of faith in the strict sense—was the cross that had to be borne by the post-Vatican II popes. They failed to do so. The two popes of "restoration," John Paul II and Benedict XVI, and Francis, the pope of "progress," were unable to maintain even the fiction of reestablished unity.

Ratzinger's attempt: framing the Council

Shortly after his election, in his well-known address to the Curia on December 22, 2005, Benedict XVI distinguished between two interpretations of the conciliar reform, "the hermeneutic of discontinuity and rupture," which he considered harmful, and "the hermeneutic of reform or renewal in continuity," which he endorsed—intended, he said, to prevent "a rupture between the preconciliar Church and the postconciliar Church." In short, the Pope defined what in a liberal democracy, to whose ways of thinking the Church is increasingly permeable, would be called a "center-right," which he legitimized, and a "center-left," which he disqualified.

There was by no means any question of his joining the traditionalist front which, in varying degrees, rejected the Council and/or the reformed liturgy. Yet, because of his interest in the preconciliar liturgy, Benedict XVI could have gone further than the hermeneutic of "renewal in continuity." His own version of "restorationism" could have become the beginning of a process of transition, like that which took place with John XXIII but in the opposite direction.

However, as we know, the process remained in the middle of the road, even with regard to "renewal in continuity": not only did it *not* lead to a rejection of the Council, but the path of restorationism, the containment (as it were) of the Council, was perceived as a failure, an attempt without decisive result. The Church in the West continued to disappear from the social space; the ecclesiastical personnel, priests, religious, seminarians, continued to diminish; the Roman center gave the impression that it no longer had a helmsman. Having become the target of continuous attacks by proponents of the "hermeneutic of discontinuity," Benedict XVI isolated himself in his private theological practice, morally anticipating the abdication he finally decided to make in 2013.

Bergoglio's attempt: maximizing the Council

As if quite naturally (but, in fact, after an intense electoral preparation), the conclave of 2013 tried the other option, the center-left one, the opposite "hermeneutic" of Vatican II, to which Jorge Bergoglio had rallied. The new pope, who in a speech to Jesuits in 2022 said he was fighting against a "restorationism" that wants to "gag" the Council, and against a "traditionalism" that wants to evacuate it, has therefore set out to "break down the walls," according to the expression he likes:

• the wall of *Humanæ Vitæ* and of the set of texts in its wake that had preserved conjugal morality from the liberalization Vatican II had brought to bear on ecclesiology: *Amoris Laetitia* declared in 2016 that people living in public adultery can remain in it without committing grave sin (*AL* 301);

• the wall of *Summorum Pontificum*, which recognized the right of the ancient liturgy, with its catechesis and clerical personnel, to serve as a "conservatory" of the Church. *Traditionis Custodes*, in 2021, and *Desiderio Desideravi*, in 2022, invalidated this attempted "return" and declared that the new liturgical books are the sole expression of the *lex orandi* of the Roman rite (*TC*, art. 1).

But the Bergoglio option is failing as the Ratzinger option had previously failed: the ecclesial institution has continued to collapse and the mission to die out. And if under Benedict XVI, disillusionment had crystallized over the lack of governance, it is now over the excess of muddled and dictatorial government—despite the watchword of synodality and despite *Prædicate Evangelium*—that critics are increasingly emerging under Francis. Moreover, just as Benedict XVI never took the risk of falling below the Council, Francis has been careful not to go beyond it at the risk of exploding an institutional structure. For example, despite all his declarations against clericalism, he has never really questioned priestly celibacy or opened the priesthood to women.

Thus, neither the attempt to soften the Council nor the attempt to maximize it has stopped the hemorrhage, which continues. It even increases, insofar as the pole of conservation (Ratzingerian and traditionalist, to sum up roughly) has become stronger. This is true, first of all, because this pole actually *grows* over time, at least through the arrival of new generations welcomed in families, whereas the progressive pole knows little transmission of this sort.

And also, because it has become a little more homogeneous, the alliance has been tightened between the Ratzingerians, supporters of a "hermeneutics of reform in continuity" and the "front of refusal," traditionalism. The latter is more present than ever, as is shown by the repeated blows that are dealt to it as if it were the enemy par excellence.

For a true reform

The adage *Ecclesia semper reformanda*, "the Church must always reform itself," dates back to the beginning of the fifteenth century, at the time of the Great Schism, when the need for a "reform in the head and in the members," in the papacy and in the whole ecclesial body, became evident to all. But it was not until more than a century later that this great desire of the Catholic world really came to fruition, beyond the reformation in the form of Protestantism's revolt, with the Council of Trent.

In fact, the theme of the reform of a Church, holy in itself but composed of sinners, dates from the eleventh century, from what historians have called the Gregorian reform—today they prefer to speak of the "Gregorian moment." Its ferment was religious life, that of Cluniac monasticism especially. It is in the objective order of things that the evangelical perfection of religious life will be the model of the necessary renovations of the Church. These are accompanied and stimulated by reforms of religious orders (among many others, we may cite that of Carmel in the sixteenth century), with a return to the demands of the Beatitudes, a spiritual and disciplinary renewal, a withdrawal from the corruption of the sinful world in order to convert oneself and to convert it (see Jn 17:16, 18: "They are not of the world, as I also am not of the world. . . . As thou hast sent me into the world, I also have sent them into the world").

However, ever since the Christianity of the Enlightenment period, in the Germanic countries, in France, and in Italy, the term "reform" began to be applied also to a quite different project: that of adapting ecclesiastical institutions to the surrounding world, which was beginning to escape from Christianity.

Two types of reform, from then on, would often find themselves in conflict: the traditional one of a reform that revitalizes the identity of the Church, and the type of reform that tries to adjust the Church to the new society in which it lives. It is essentially the traditional idea of reform that was found in such movements as the rebirth of religious orders, especially Benedictine, in the nineteenth century after the revolutionary turmoil, the Thomistic restoration beginning with Leo XIII, the liturgical and disciplinary reforms of St. Pius X at the beginning of the twentieth century, and the attempts at a doctrinal and liturgical containment of the great ebullition of the 1950s by Pius XII. On the contrary, the adaptive idea of reform, with its programmatic book *Vraie et fausse réforme dans l'Église* [*True and False Reform in the Church*] by Yves Congar (Cerf, 1950), can be read in the "new theology" of the post-war years, in the ecumenical movement and, to some extent, in (at least the later phase of) the Liturgical Movement; it triumphed with Vatican II.

An ecclesiological reversal

A reform of the Gregorian type, with a rediscovered liturgy, a rigorous discipline, a demanding formation of the candidates for the priesthood, a holy and strong stature of the pastors, a reevangelization through a recatechization, goes hand-in-hand with an ecclesiological reversal.

But is it not pure fantasy to wish for a return to a Church of the "Gregorian moment" type, when the state of our Mother, half a century after Vatican II (and to a large extent because of this Council) is in a state of maximum dereliction, without any capacity to assert the "triumphalist" claims that are attributed to the papacy of the eleventh century?

Certainly not, if we consider that God's strength is first deployed in weakness. The weakness here is extreme—that of a Catholicism more and more anomalous for the surrounding culture. And very weak is also what, in spite of everything, continues to flourish in it and which it is difficult to imagine as the crucible of a spiritual, catechetical, missionary, vocational renewal, but which can nonetheless participate in it. In its present state, what is called the "new Catholicism," made up of priests who look and act like priests, young faithful, seriously practicing families, new communities, traditionalisms of all sensibilities: *this represents in the West all that will remain alive in a few years.* Its numerical importance is very small and it has, moreover, the greatest difficulty in resisting the weight of modernity, the impregnation of a devastating individualism, and the "bourgeois" temptation which presses upon it.

What kind of reform tomorrow? "When I am weak, then I am strong" (2 Cor 12:10). And to return to Rome and its Curia, is it necessary, or even possible, for the Successor of Peter to continue to appear as a kind of universal leader? In a great "infirmity" (to speak as St. Paul did), what constitutes the *essence* of the Roman and universal episcopate—namely, the fact of speaking the Faith in the name of Christ without the possibility of deviating—could appear as the pure gold that remains at the bottom of the sieve of the crisis.

2

The Celebration of Divorce*

CHRISTIAN BROWNE

Rorate Caeli
October 24, 2022

FEW OTHER OCCURENCES IN HISTORY HAVE THEIR achievements celebrated as often as does the Second Vatican Council. So, although rather tiresome, the laudatory commemoration of the sixtieth anniversary of the opening of the Council is *de rigueur* for today's rather tiresome ecclesial establishment. Worthy of note, however, is the defensive tone adopted for the birthday party in which the Council's partisans have made a point to defend the Council *ab initio*—insisting that it was necessary to hold the Council and that it was, in conception, a great and a good moment in history—one that remains untarnished by, and even divorced from, its aftermath.

Those who see the Council in this manner are, for the most part, Baby Boomers (e.g., George Weigel) and members of the generation that preceded the Boomers (what name shall we give the generation that produced Bergoglio, Biden, and Pelosi?). For this cohort, the Council was the New Frontier for Religion. Just as the political torch was passed to a new generation in the wake of the disasters of the first half of the twentieth century, so too the Council would usher in a new age of Catholicism that would surpass reliance upon morality manuals and the stale memorization of Scholastic conceptions and rules. It was the moonshot for the Church.

It is easy to mock or scorn this view now, but, in proper perspective, these notions are understandable. The mid-century desire for

---

* Original title: "Lofty concepts and great hopes cannot be separated, in practical judgment, from their effects."

renewal, for a more Scriptural and Christocentric expression of the Faith, was legitimate. It was also legitimate to address the Church's relationship to the modern States, deeply scarred as it was by more than two hundred years of revolution and uneasy coexistence. Putting aside the impossible-to-answer question of the Council's "necessity," it was not inherently absurd or nefarious to wish to take up these matters in an effort to strengthen the Church's spiritual and political life.

The defenders of the convoking of the Council still feel profoundly the "dream" of this revivified and dynamic Christianity. What they wanted (they plead) was good and noble, just as the architects of the Great Society would say they were driven by the desire to eliminate poverty, hunger, and ignorance. But these lofty concepts and great hopes, while laudable in themselves, cannot be separated in practical judgment from their effects—from the results that these efforts caused in reality.

The Great Society did not eliminate poverty, hunger, and ignorance. Its results are mixed and complex—it achieved some good results, but also caused unintended negative consequences that continue to haunt our political and economic life. The Council did not achieve its ends, either, and its bizarre and disastrous "implementation" cannot be separated from its history. Although a factually inaccurate conflation, the Council by now has been nearly identified with the Novus Ordo and all the changes to Catholic life and practice that came in its wake.

Thus, the defense of Council's commencement, its documents, or what this or that bishop really said, retains at this point only an intellectual appeal; as a practical matter these sorts of points mean nothing, because they came to nothing. We know that the Council did not order the elimination of Latin in the Mass and the implementation of Communion in the hand. We get it. But these things happened after the Council and were done in its name. The present pope and his curial officials invoke the Council as the infallible authority for all that has come after it. To question or critique these postconciliar practices is to reject the Council, we are told!

Sadly, the defense of the Council *per se*, therefore, becomes nothing more than an effort at historical accuracy. It tries to explain (usually in the best light possible) why the Council was thought necessary and the lofty goals of (some) of its participants, but it has almost zero practical application for the resolution of the roiling crisis that the Council unleashed.

These efforts also ignore the "lived experience" of the generations that came of age in the Council's aftermath. The preconciliar generations were the beneficiaries of the old system, with its stability and intellectual rigor; its reliance on the widespread presence of priests and religious; and its ability to exert great spiritual and academic influence on those with whom it came in contact.

The generations that followed the Council—like mine—encountered a completely changed landscape. When I was awakened to the Faith at the age of fourteen, I knew nothing about Vatican II or the Latin Mass. But from the first, I felt instinctively that something was amiss in the Church that I loved. I saw the great and unused marble altar affixed to the wall of our high school chapel with a Latin inscription above it; I saw old yearbook photos of the many Jesuits in their cassocks; the boys kneeling at the daily Mass; the emphasis on classical learning; the Sodality of Our Lady. I knew, by a sort of *sensus fidelium*, that the guitars and the hand-holding and the felt banners and the bad hymns were alien to the Church.

Certainly, I was not *taught* to believe that; on the contrary. Yet, looking back, for me and for those few of my generation who retained the Faith, I feel as if we were travelers, returning home after a long journey, to find the ruins of a once-great civilization—unable to understand why, exactly, our forefathers had torn down and abandoned its great halls and magnificent temples.

Put crudely, as a practical matter, I do not care why John XXIII called the Council. I do not care about the dreams of its *periti* or the inspiration it gave to Catholic schoolboys under the tutelage of nuns whose orders would be eviscerated a few years later. I do not subscribe to the ideological effort to suppress reality, for it is this effort that prevents the Church from fairly and justly judging its past—praising what is praiseworthy, but discarding that which is harmful or the product of false and misplaced hopes.

A metaphor comes to mind from the world of great public architecture. The demolition of Pennsylvania Station in New York began in 1963. The grand railway station, more splendid even than Grand Central Terminal, was too expensive to keep up. It was, moreover, a relic. The days of railroad travel were ending. It was no longer needed, and progress demanded that it give way to a new, modern Madison Square Garden. Time marches on; the needs of society change.

Penn Station still exists today. It is there, buried beneath Seventh Avenue. It is a functioning railroad station, the busiest in North America. Ten of thousands pass through it every day. And it is, undoubtedly, the most reviled public space in the City of New York.

The allure of progress is powerful, but, like the unclean spirit gone out of the man only to return with seven more, it can leave its object in worse condition than that in which it was found. There is a place *called* Penn Station where people board trains, but the retention of the name, the function and the location does not, in reality, mean that Penn Station still exists. It was torn down, to the shame of those who allowed such vandalism. The only relevant, practical question for those who loved its beauty is whether it can ever be rebuilt.

3

Getting the Joke:
The Last Act of Vatican II

MADOC CAIRNS

florilegium
November 9, 2022

AN APHORISM OF IVAN ILLICH: "THE CHRISTIAN IS THE one who gets the joke."

There's a moment in Louis Bouyer's memoirs that, I think, expresses it near-perfectly. Bouyer—a bespectacled, cultured intellectual—has spent years dodging reactionary Bishops, philistine manualists who think the slightest hint of reform is blasphemy *in se*. He's on the outside. Then comes Vatican II. Bouyer is named *peritus*, theological advisor. He helps draft council documents, sits on key committees. Reform gets a seat at the table.

But after the council, Bouyer finds himself in trouble again. Everywhere he goes, Bishops are rewriting catechisms, tearing up their cathedrals, abandoning things the council praised, introducing things it never mentioned. They look at Bouyer with suspicion. At best they see him as a relic; at worst as a renegade. In neither case is he welcome. He finds himself, once again, on the outside.

Here's the punchline: *the Bishops were the same.*

Unregenerate neoscholastics morphed, neatly and without obvious discomfort, into ardent progressives. Old wine had found new wineskins. The grand inquisitor had taken an enneagram test. On one level, Bouyer realised, everything in the Church had changed. On quite another, nothing had. He got the joke.

The ongoing debate about Vatican II is wrong-headed, I think, for exactly this reason. People look to the council for "continuity" or for "rupture." They should be looking for the joke.

Getting the Joke: The Last Act of Vatican II

How's this one: it's overwhelmingly likely that most of the Bishops at Vatican II were complicit in covering up the abuse of children. In fact, based on what we now know, we can go further. Covering up child abuse was one of the great unifiers of the conciliar Church.

Rembert Weakland and Bernard Law, Marcial Maciel and Jean Vanier, Steubenville and Schoenstatt: these men—and it was, is, almost always men—differed on practically everything. But when it came to covering up abuse, to perpetuating it, *they were the same.*

If you're looking for the key ecclesiological event of the twentieth century, or the defining experience of twenty-first-century Catholicism, or the critical axis around which the Church will orientate itself for the foreseeable future, it's not Vatican II you're looking for. It's the abuse crisis.

Both interpretations of the council—liberal and conservative, reform and restoration—are failures. Worse: they're dead. This doesn't mean that the changes the council made, or the changes the conciliar papacies implemented, are going to disappear. But little meaningful change can nowadays be expected on either end of the spectrum, because Catholic Christianity ultimately has only one agent of reform: Bishops.

And nowadays Bishops have no authority beyond what the faithful freely grant them. In practice, if not in theology, theirs is a purely moral authority, a relationship founded on trust as well as duty. And that trust, that authority—that relationship—no longer exists. Do you really owe holy obedience to men who cover up the abuse of children?

It will take a long time for this to filter through to the upper echelons of the Church, clerical and lay. If you're old enough to see the abuse crisis as a crisis rather than a norm, you can rely upon the instincts of tribalism and obedience that made Catholics Catholic. If you're young, you have to live in the world those instincts made.

Last week, I went to a lecture by George Weigel, who has a new book out on Vatican II.[1] It was exactly what you'd expect—JP2 good, liberals bad—but carried with it, I thought, an extraordinary

---

1. See chapters 21 and 22.

sense of anachronism; as if the whole thing was being delivered from twenty years in the past. We no longer live in the world of good and bad bishops. We live in the world where, on the issue that really mattered, *they were the same.*

All things considered, it was a bravura performance from Weigel, standing high in the stirrups, an old soldier with battles still to fight. Walking out from the hall into the rain, it occurred to me that someone should tell him to lay down his arms. The New Evangelisation and the New Pentecost share a common grave now. The war is over. Everyone lost.

But there's not much you could say to that, really, especially not in a public lecture. Except, perhaps, this: Funny joke. *Ha, Ha, Ha.*

4

The Most Fruitless Search

PHILIP CAMPBELL

Unam Sanctam Catholicum
October 24, 2022

THERE IS A MOMENT OF EPIPHANY ON THE ROAD TO traditionalism that occurs when you realize that the progressive junta that controls the Church does not actually care what Vatican II taught.

I remember my mindset before this earthshaking revelation. I recall arguing that what we needed was "fidelity to the conciliar documents," getting back to "what Vatican II really taught." I used to post essays exegeting the conciliar documents in an attempt to show "what they really mean." I was fully aboard the Weigelian Express, hoping, ever vainly, for a "*real* implementation of the Council." I thought patient explanation of the "real meaning" of these documents was a sufficient response to the Modernist crisis; that the reason priests and bishops allowed nonsense unchecked throughout their churches was because they honestly didn't know that *Sacrosanctum Concilium* called for the preservation of Latin and chant, or sincerely didn't understand the real meaning of *participatio actuosa*.

But for how many years can one exhaust himself in such pursuits? How long can one beat one's head against the wall? To be sure, it is important to understand the documents from a theological perspective; but it is another thing if we think that patiently explaining the documents in hopes that the "real Council" will emerge is anything other than chasing an elusive will-o'-the-wisp.

At a certain point I realized—as many of us have—that the progressives don't care what Vatican II said. They don't view the Council as a series of teachings; rather, they view it as an event. And not just any event, but an event whose nature is metahistorical. It is not merely another step in the long path of historical development; it is a paradigm-shattering upheaval that breaks the fourth wall of history, purporting not only to change the historical trajectory of the Church but to remove the Church entirely from the bounds of history and tradition. What do people with such lofty visions, such grandiose pretensions, care about the precise definition of *participatio actuosa,* the rubrics of the *General Instruction of the Roman Missal,* or any other considerations that are merely textual?

Six years ago, I was invited to the home of a mainstream Catholic apologist to deliver a talk on the role of Catholic Tradition. Therein I argued—as I still argue today—that treating the Council like a collection of texts while failing to understand it as an historical event is the principal reason why "conservatives" make no headway against the progressive revolution. After the talk, one of the attendees, a notable hyperpapalist theologian, just kept shaking his head in disagreement, saying, "No, no, the documents matter!" as if it were a mantra. This fellow has been rightly lambasted in traditional Catholic outlets recently for ridiculous attempts to square the circle concerning *Traditionis Custodes.* Six years later, he's still shaking his head and repeating the mantra.

When speaking of Sacred Scripture, St. Thomas Aquinas says we can have a meaningful disputation with an opponent only if he admits some of the truths of revelation. "Against those who deny one article of faith," he says, "we can argue from another." But what if the opponent does not grant any of the articles of divine revelation? Then argument becomes impossible, as there is no common ground, for, he continues, "if our opponent believes nothing of divine revelation, there is no longer any means of proving the articles of faith by reasoning, but only of answering his objections."[1]

Similarly, if it has become clear that progressives don't grant any stable authority to the texts of Vatican II, then upon what common ground can we stand? Upon what foundation do we plant our feet when we presume to uncover "what the Council *really* said" to our opponents who do not care? We are not dealing with two different

1. *Summa theologiae* I, Q. 1, art. 8.

hermeneutical approaches to conciliar documents, but with two different paradigms of the Council itself, between which there is a vast chasm fixed, that those who would pass from the one side to the other might not be able.

I can hear some objecting, "Trads don't grant authority to the texts of Vatican II either!" It is true that we do not grant it *infallible* authority, but this is hardly novel; it is nothing beyond what Paul VI himself taught, when he said:

> There are those who ask what authority, what theological qualification, the Council intended to give to its teachings, knowing that it avoided issuing solemn dogmatic definitions backed by the Church's infallible teaching authority. The answer is known by those who remember the conciliar declaration of March 6, 1964, repeated on November 16, 1964. In view of the pastoral nature of the Council, it avoided proclaiming in an extraordinary manner any dogmata carrying the mark of infallibility.[2]

Traditional Catholics are in fact the *only* segment of the Church attempting to construct an accurate interpretation of Vatican II, in terms of both the documents' meaning and their authority. While understanding that the documents are only part of the phenomenon known as Vatican II, we still affirm they have an objective content that should at least be understood.

This is totally contrary to the progressive manner of utilizing the documents. Examples are legion, but let's take a recent article from *America* magazine wherein a Jesuit cardinal waxes eloquent about the Amazon's newly approved "ecclesial conferences" that will replace the regional episcopal conference.[3] These new conferences will incorporate lay people—men and women—in the governance of the Church. The cardinal says this arrangement "stems from the Second Vatican Council" and cites *Lumen Gentium* in justification. *Lumen Gentium* says nothing about lay people governing the

---

2. Pope Paul VI, General Audience of January 12, 1966.

3. See Gerard O'Connell, "In historic first, Pope Francis approves an 'ecclesial conference' with lay people instead of a bishops-only leadership body," *America*, October 3, 2022, www.americamagazine.org/faith/2022/10/03/amazon-ecclesial-con ference-pope-francis-243891.

Church; it specifically says that the bishops rule the Church by divine decree, and that lay people participate in the work of God through their secular work and family life. The cardinal doesn't care what Vatican II teaches. "Vatican II" becomes a meaningless label assigned to any and every novelty.

The ridiculous novelties the Vatican is churning out faster than the Fed churns out US dollars are more likely these days to elicit my laughter than my consternation. To be sure, I am deeply saddened and appalled at the state of my Holy Mother Church, but there is only so much a person can stand up to before his battleworn face cracks into a smile, then breaks forth into laughter at the nonsense of it all. It is a strange but proper human response to absurdity, especially in situations where the severity of it has escalated to the point of ridiculousness. Saddle me with a ten thousand dollar debt and I will be concerned; saddle me with a ten million dollar debt and I am more likely to laugh in your face.

There is no more useless endeavor than to search for "*the real Vatican II.*" One has a better chance finding the Fountain of Youth or the Ark of the Covenant. That's because there is no "real Vatican II" that can be found by documentary analysis alone, and it is a most fruitless search to think otherwise. Vatican II can't be found solely in the documents any more than the French Revolution can be found by reading the *Declaration of the Rights of Man.*

And so, I no longer engage in intellectual hand-wringing over the "real meaning" of Vatican II. I certainly acknowledge an objective meaning of the documents, and I am even capable of expounding it if I've had enough to drink. But I have long since jumped off the Weigelian Express, preferring rather to walk in "the ancient paths where the good way is" (Jer 6:16), even if I move at a snail's pace, for I prefer the exile of the desert to the plunge off the precipice of irrelevance for which the "real council" railcar is heading.

5

A Victim of Its Own Success[*]

LARRY CHAPP

Our Sunday Visitor
October 7, 2022

THIS YEAR WE ARE CELEBRATING THE SIXTIETH ANNI-versary of the opening of the Second Vatican Council (1962–1965). The question of the council's legacy is an ongoing matter of continuing debate among theologians whose discussions of the finer theological points of the council leave most average Catholics yawning. The relationship between nature and grace? What is that? Neoscholasticism versus more modern theologies? Hmmm... don't really understand theology anyway, so who cares? Religious freedom for all in civil society? Duh, isn't that a no-brainer? Non-Catholics have a legit shot at salvation? Well, of course they do. Mass in the vernacular in a reformed liturgy? Is that still a question for anyone other than a small group of right-wing Latin fanatics over at that abandoned parish downtown? Local bishops now have more independent authority from the pope than they did before? Really? Seems the pope is still the celebrity center of attention with the Catholic media reporting on the pope's every hiccup and facial twitch.

Thus, the deeper question, beyond all of the ongoing theological debates, is why an average Catholic in the pews should continue to care about the council at all since it seems now to be in our rearview mirrors as "your grandfather's council," lacking any real existential grip on the day-to-day concerns of average people. The cultural

---

[*] Original title: "Sixty years after the opening of the Second Vatican Council, where do we stand?" From *Our Sunday Visitor*, October 7, 2022 © Our Sunday Visitor Publishing. www.osv.com. Used by permission.

thought-world of the early '60s seems so foreign to us now, with the concerns of that distant time now residing as a mere caricature in our minds lumped together with vague memories of hippies, drugs, Vietnam and the Beatles. And so we can perhaps be excused for a certain indifference to the whole affair. After all, aren't there even perfectly orthodox theologians who are now saying that the council's moment has passed and we need a Vatican III to set things right and to take up more contemporary concerns? Aren't there disgruntled traditional Catholics out there who blame the council for all of the Church's modern woes and say that we should now just ignore it as a failure? And aren't there a bunch of liberal Catholics in the Church today in increasing numbers who say that we should just move on from the council and embrace the modern world's progressive agenda, especially in matters of morality?

All of these observations are true, and to the extent that the average Catholic is aware of such things—no matter how vaguely—there is an understandable intellectual and spiritual exhaustion concerning the council that can only breed a certain frustration that we are fixated on a now distantly past ecclesial event to the detriment of addressing the real needs of today. Should we not instead be focused on why there are so few religious vocations, why our children are walking away from the Faith in droves, why so many parishes and schools are closing, and why we still can't seem to come to grips with the fallout from the sex abuse crisis? Is not a concern over the council directly analogous to Nero fiddling as Rome burned around him? Most Catholics today, I think, would answer that last question in the affirmative, even as they continue to question the credibility of their shepherds who seem more focused today on financial and managerial concerns than on the more fundamental question of why anyone should continue to believe at all.

A new claim

Nevertheless, and despite the heartfelt legitimacy of all of these issues, my claim is exactly the opposite. In my view, the council has been a victim here of its own success. Yes, you heard that right. The council was, and contrary to the reigning narrative, a success and not a failure. There is a sad tendency these days to focus on all of the turmoil that happened in the wake of the council and to use that turmoil as the primary metric for assessing the success of the conciliar project. But I think this is a deeply problematic way of assessing the council and is flawed on multiple levels.

First, if you know even a little Church history, then you are undoubtedly aware that many of the Church's most important and consequential councils created enormous controversy and turmoil in their wake. Just think of the very first ecumenical council of the Church, the council of Nicaea (325), which was called by the freshly minted Christian, Emperor Constantine, in order to combat the groundswell of support for what is now known as the Arian heresy. "Arianism" (named after the priest Arius) was, in a nutshell, the theological assertion that Christ is not coequal to the Father in divinity but is instead a "creature" like other creatures, albeit the highest creature in the hierarchy of God's creation. It was a powerful and popular heresy since it fit so well into the then-reigning platonic cosmological/philosophical paradigm. In other words, it was a theology perfectly tailored to reflect the "spirit" of the times, which accounts for its wild popularity among the clergy in particular. But Nicaea condemned this theology and affirmed that Christ was "consubstantial" with the Father, which was just a fancy metaphysical term meant to affirm that Christ is equal in divinity to the Father. It then issued the famous Nicene Creed that we still recite at every Sunday Mass and high holy days some 1700 years later.

So, case settled, right? Wrong. There were still influential bishops and Roman authorities who refused to accept the conciliar definitions, and the great debate raged on for many more decades and was not really completely resolved for another century or more. And think of poor St. Athanasius, a tireless champion of Nicene orthodoxy, who faced relentless persecution and exile for his steadfast support of the full divinity of Christ. And it took several more ecumenical councils over several more centuries to completely flesh out the full significance of the Nicene affirmations, which required the development of whole new theological and philosophical categories that were also controversial in their own right, setting off raging debates that continued on for centuries and that even led some churches to break away into schism over what they believed were the "novelties" of the preceding councils. St. Maximus the Confessor (ca. 580–662), centuries after Nicaea, was persecuted for his defense of the various conciliar affirmations concerning Christ, and was put on trial for heresy in Constantinople, which eventually led to his tongue being cut out and his right hand (his writing hand) being cut off so that he would cease his activities of preaching and writing. He died shortly thereafter.

Compared to such turmoil and persecutions, the conciliar mayhem after Vatican II looks positively pale and tame in comparison. It is, therefore, laughable from a strictly historical perspective that a mere sixty years of controversy and debate should be used as an argument against the "success" of Vatican II. Furthermore, we see that the postconciliar chaos was caused by the exact same social forces that caused the problems after Nicaea—namely, that there were many in the Church who wanted the Church to conform to the cultural and moral norms of the current culture as well as the philosophical ideologies that animated that culture. It is a story as old as the Church herself, as we see in the letters of St. Paul as he struggled to get his congregations to stop thinking like Roman pagans and trying to fit Christ into that matrix.

What average Catholics need

My point in all of this is to point out that even if we feel a certain exhaustion over the council, we must not allow ourselves to become so jaded to the controversies that we just throw up our hands and throw in the towel. Like it or not, Vatican II was the most important Catholic event of modern times, and despite the disagreements over its meaning—and despite our fatigue over those disagreements— we must not allow ourselves to succumb to the temptation of a weariness that causes our devotion to its message to wane. What if Athanasius or Maximus had thought this way? Had they given up the cause, the Church would have suffered even greater indignities and distortions that would have taken several more centuries than it already did to sort out. Likewise for us, since if we were to just give up on the council now, we would be turning the Church over to those very forces that distorted its message in the first place, which would set us back even further.

A Victim of Its Own Success

The "average Catholic," of course, does not think in these kinds of categories, and it therefore falls upon our shepherds to be more diligent in explaining it all to us, so that the average Catholic can, indeed, come to appreciate what is at stake in these debates. Because what may appear to the regular Catholic in the pews as nothing more than an arcane theological exercise in hair-splitting is, in fact, something of tremendous importance—as important in its own way as the theological hair-splitting at Nicaea, which, though far removed from the ordinary discourse of ordinary Christians, was of world-changing significance that altered forever the course of history, both secular and sacred. Theology might be dull to most, and it might seem a nerdy form of discourse among pin-headed, geeky intellectuals, but it is of central importance to the Church, and the laity must, therefore, be taught theology by her shepherds in a way that theological language is transformed into the language of evangelical witness.

It can be done and has been done, and so the rejoinder that this is impossible is demonstrably false. Just look at the success of Bishop Robert Barron's Word on Fire materials that are extremely popular among rank-and-file Catholics. This also goes to show that there is an opposite error very prevalent among many theologians and shepherds who assume that the laity cannot handle such things and then infantilize the laity with boring and anodyne homilies filled with "stories" and jokes—homilies that never rise to the level of a serious challenge or intellectual provocation. Because the fact is, there are millions and millions of educated modern Catholics who are exposed to this boring form of Catholicism and who then compare it to their educated and sophisticated knowledge of any number of topics, and they find that the Faith by comparison seems childish and utterly superficial. And this is true as well for very young Catholics who can handle far more theological sophistication than we give them credit for and who are actually starved for a Church that is deeper and more profound, and, therefore, more interesting. I cannot tell you how many times when I was still a professor of theology that I would finish a class and have droves of students say to me, "Why is this the first time I am hearing this? Why has this never been taught to me? This is wonderful!"

And all of this has a direct bearing on the ongoing significance of the council and why average Catholics should still care about it.

Successes of the council

I spoke earlier of the council being a success, in spite of the many deviations from orthodoxy and sanity that followed in its wake, and it is important to point out those successes in order for us to appreciate them and build upon them. Take, for example, my own profession—theology—and notice how the council, in many good ways, changed theology forever to such an extent that there can no longer be any question of going back to a preconciliar form of theology, which, though having many salutary attributes, had become moribund and deficient. Think, too, of the fact that I, a layperson, was allowed into the theological guild at all, since before the council, theology was almost exclusively the playpen for priests and bishops. I have many hypertraditionalist lay theologian friends who routinely trash the council and who write many books on that topic but who fail to notice that, prior to the very same council, they would not have had the chance to do so. In other words, they are a living witness to the success of a council they so easily dismiss as a failure.

There is also the fact that Mass is now in the vernacular language of the people, which I think is a very good thing. And even if the modern liturgy could use some reforming, the fact remains that it was because of the council that we can all now pray the liturgy in our mother tongues instead of sitting back, as so many did before the council, and let the priest do his thing while we prayed a Rosary. It is also a good thing that Catholics, because of the council, are able to embrace the concept of religious freedom and to, therefore, view evangelization as a noncoercive enterprise of proposing the Gospel that is also the responsibility of us all and not just something for missionaries in some far-off land.

In other words, we must not allow the successes of the council to seem like "obvious things that would have happened anyway" and, because that is not true, we must further realize that there is still much work to be done and still a great danger that those successes will be lost by our own inaction and indifference to what is still at stake. Because, make no mistake, there are forces at work in the Church today—both on the right and on the left—that want nothing more than to destroy those conciliar successes. Therefore, if we adopt an insouciant attitude of indifference we may wake up someday soon to a Church we do not recognize. And then we will all wonder, "what happened?" and scratch our heads in disbelief over the sad state of affairs that has come upon us.

Universal call to holiness

But there is one aspect of the council, central to its message and mission, that remains woefully underdeveloped and is one of the primary causes of many of the postconciliar pastoral failures. And that is the council's emphasis on the universal call to holiness as an absolutely essential aspect of what the Church must be in the modern world. And this is also the primary reason why average Catholics who do care deeply for the Faith should still view the council as an event of deep and ongoing significance. The council was a missionary council, as Pope St. Paul VI and every pope since has emphasized. The council made many noteworthy advances in theology and doctrine, but it was all done with an eye toward rejuvenating the Church's evangelizing efforts in the modern world. The council fathers understood that the often legalistic and superficial "contractual Catholicism" of the Church of that time had led to an infantilized laity who tended to view the whole enterprise as an effort in "following the rules" established by the hierarchy. And the council further understood, given the democratic nature of modern society and the diminution of respect for authority and hierarchy—especially religious authority and hierarchy—that going forward, evangelization could no longer be confined to the ranks of the clergy and that the laity needed to be energized and empowered to take the Gospel into the world and to leaven that world with its message.

However, there is an old Latin phrase: *Nemo dat quod non habet*. This means, "you cannot give away what you do not rightfully possess." Therefore, in order for the laity to be able to "give away" the Gospel message, they themselves had to live it with more evangelical fervor and, indeed, with a certain radicality in order to "rightfully possess" the very thing they need to share.

Sadly, instead of this message of a universal call to holiness, what we got instead in the popular Catholicism, put forward in the media and by many priests and bishops in the postconciliar era, was a message of accommodation to the values of the modern world. The conciliar call to "open the windows of the Church" and to go out into the world with the Gospel morphed instead into a Church that allowed the culture to blow in like a hurricane. The message that you can find holiness even in doing ordinary things was then transformed into its opposite: namely, that it is holy to be ordinary. After that happened, the rout was on and the bottom fell out of this most central of conciliar ambitions.

We can debate forever why this happened, and that is an important debate to have, but one thing is certain: The council as such was not the cause of the debacle but its victim. And I make that claim with full knowledge of those who think the opposite.

Therefore, even if the average Catholic may not know it, the council remains significant insofar as its gains and successes need to be solidified, and that means the laity need to take up the unfinished conciliar business of seriously seeking the path of holiness. And I will further add that this is no longer an option for us but, rather, a necessity. Cultural Catholicism is dead. And the forces within modern culture are all lined up against the message of the Gospel. Therefore, a lukewarm, halfway-house Catholicism that merely drifts with that culture will not hold, as all of the current statistics about Church affiliation bear out. For every new Catholic entering the Church, there are seven who leave. It should be quite clear, therefore, that only an intentional Catholicism, fully embraced and seriously lived out, will survive.

C. S. Lewis once compared modern Christians to eggs and said that, like an egg, we must either hatch or go bad. Choosing to stand where we are without transformation is no longer an option. Therefore, the ongoing significance of Vatican II is clear. It is the time for the laity to hatch and to spark a revolution of the heart at the center of the Church.

6

The Council is Here to Stay, and Righly So*

LARRY CHAPP

Catholic World Report
October 15, 2022

EVERYBODY I KNOW SEEMS TO BE WRITING SOMETHING on Vatican II these days and I began feeling a bit left out of the fun. So, I thought I would jump into the mosh pit of pundits to offer my take. The many recent commentaries, if I'm allowed the chutzpah to summarize them, fall into five basic categories.

First, there is the view that Vatican II was a wonderful Council in full continuity with the tradition. But it was implemented poorly and hijacked by progressives, who made liberal use of the mass media to spread the view that the Council was about liberalizing the Church in a culturally accommodationist direction. This is the approach taken by a great many "conservative" theologians whose primary aim, it seems to me, is to establish that the Council was not in any way a rupture with the past and that the vast ecclesial ruptures that ensued were solely the product of extraconciliar forces that could not have been anticipated. This view, however, is marred by the fact it is too convenient and tidy. It is a revisionist and romanticized reading of a conciliar event that was far more contentious than such a narrative of deep and smooth continuity implies.

Second, there is the traditionalist view, growing in popularity, that the Council, though not in explicit doctrinal error, was nevertheless riddled with ambiguities. These ambiguities were caused by the need for compromise between the warring conciliar factions

---

* Original title: "Vatican II: Five views sixty years on."

which allowed enough loopholes to exist for the aforementioned progressive takeover of the postconciliar interpretive spin to succeed. Furthermore, since the Council was by its own self-definition meant to be a pastoral Council, the disaster that followed can only mean that the conciliar project was, by definition, a failure. Therefore, the Council is best ignored until a future pope can correct those ambiguities and/or simply exercise a kind of line-item veto power to eliminate the troublesome bits entirely. This approach, like the first, has the benefit of a clean simplicity. But the idea that we can suppress an entire ecumenical council just because it generated controversy and confusion in its wake flies in the face of how councils have historically played out.

Third, and somewhat related to the second view, there are those who point out that the Council is now simply out of date insofar as the culture it sought to engage and evangelize no longer exists. This seems to be the view of Eric Sammons at *Crisis Magazine*, who argues that it is now time to "retire" the Council as an enterprise for an era whose moment has passed.[1] This view tends to ignore the particular theological achievements of the Council and fixates instead on the Council's general pastoral aims, which it deems to be outmoded. This is a clever act of legerdemain, despite the partial truthfulness of its central claim, since it reductively associates the Council with purely pragmatic and proximate concerns, allowing the restorationist wing of the Church to summarily dismiss the Council without for all that appearing to be hostile to it.

Fourth, there is the view that in allowing the ressourcement theologians (e.g., Joseph Ratzinger, Henri de Lubac, et al.) to set the agenda and to scuttle the already prepared schemata, the Council imprudently marginalized the standard Thomistic ecclesial theology up to that point. This destroyed the Church's theological unity and inner coherence, and replaced it with nothing more than a loose aggregate of various scholars whose overall body of work did not provide the Church with the tools it needed for a proper postconciliar implementation of the Council's main pastoral aims. In other words, the Council privileged innovative and speculative the-

1. See chapter 19.

ologies over the development of a standard theology, resulting in the loss of a common theological frame of reference.

This approach, articulated brilliantly in 2007 by Rusty Reno at *First Things*,[2] acknowledges the great value and contribution of the ressourcement school of theologians. But it views their theology as a one-off "heroic generation" kind of thing that cannot be reduplicated now because those theologians only made sense within the context of the standard Thomistic theology that they so bitterly rejected. Their theology was bold, exploratory, and breathtaking in its synthetic alacrity with all manner of ideas, but all of it emerged out of the thought world and vocabulary of the standard theology—a theology we no longer possess. Therefore, as Reno notes, the great paradox is that modern students of theology can no longer appreciate the contributions of the heroic generation because they have no frame of reference for the debates that those theologians were engaged in. Ressourcement killed the neoscholastic dragon, but in so doing laid waste to the only possible context for understanding its own constructions. And the Council, insofar as it eschewed neoscholasticism in favor of ressourcement thinkers, likewise scuttled its own project.

This brings us to the final approach, which, building on the view espoused by Reno and others, now seeks to recover elements of that old Thomistic synthesis and to thereby recover as well the full contextual significance of the ressourcement thinkers. Well aware that the Council was indeed a ressourcement affair, this approach understands that the Council itself therefore needs to be historically contextualized as the fruit of a set of theological debates that began in the nineteenth century and picked up full steam in the twentieth century. It understands that those debates were often acrimonious, leading the neoscholastics to demonize the ressourcement thinkers as dangerous modernist saboteurs obsessed with subjectivity and historicity, and the ressourcement thinkers to return the favor by counter-punching the neoscholastic "bullies" with accusations of intellectual stupor and superficiality. And things were made even

2. "Theology after the Revolution," *First Things*, May 2007, online at www.firstthings.com/article/2007/05/theology-after-the-revolution.

more heated owing to the often censorious and oppressive role played by the Holy Office as it moved against ressourcement thinkers such as de Lubac whose own Jesuit order silenced him. This was not an atmosphere of irenic and collegial debate and this historical acrimony spilled over into the Council itself, with the ressourcement school emerging as victors and the neoscholastics, sadly, in full retreat.

Therefore, this view correctly seeks to interpret the Council, despite its self-definition as a pastoral Council, as primarily a theological event dominated by the debates between the Thomistic old guard and the young ressourcement Turks. The theologian Matthew Levering is a brilliant expositor of this approach and he interprets the Council positively as a profound theological event that deepened the interconnectivity between ecclesiology and Christology—a deepening that had across-the-board implications for a large number of theological issues. Therefore, Levering has an astute appreciation for the innovative genius of the ressourcement theologians as well as a deep awareness of the Council's true legacy as a theological event of great and enduring significance. We have barely scratched the surface of those implications and therefore the Council's enduring legacy is, ironically, the unfinished nature of the theological renewal it generated. But that renewal was shortcircuited by the wholesale rejection of the preconciliar standard theology which gave it its context. As Reno notes, even great ressourcement theologians like Balthasar and de Lubac, after the postconciliar mayhem took root, began to lament in highly polemical terms the loss of a standard ecclesial culture as the progressive innovators took advantage of the loss of the old Thomistic synthesis.

To his credit, Levering, along with careful and historically conscious scholars like Matthew Minerd, are attempting a rejuvenation of that renewal via a retrieval of the lost treasures of preconciliar Thomism and the fusing together of those treasures with the ressourcement theologians. Their project is a bold one since they are attempting to restructure the entire debate surrounding the Council within the totality of its theological/historical context and to thereby point us beyond a mere hermeneutics of the Council and toward a genuine retrieval of its project by actually developing that project further. Therefore, it is both diagnostic and prescriptive, and it offers a true opportunity at a rapprochement between schools of thought that should be natural allies against the common enemy of a corrosively acidic progressivism rather than enemies.

The legitimacy of this approach's insights can be readily seen when we look at how Thomistic many of the ressourcement thinkers actually were. De Lubac was a great retriever of the Fathers to be sure, but it was often done with an eye toward a more fulsome understanding of Aquinas and his theology of nature and grace in particular. And much of de Lubac's career was spent in debates over Thomas's views on that topic. Balthasar quoted Aquinas more than any other author and structured his trilogy around the classical scholastic formulation of the transcendental properties of Being (One, True, Good, Beautiful). He also held that the greatest breakthrough in the history of philosophy was Aquinas's metaphysical insight about the real distinction between essence and existence. Rahner was deeply indebted to scholastic categories even as he moved beyond them in his Catholic Kantianism, for better or for worse. Lonergan, a neglected genius, was deeply informed by Thomistic categories of thought. I could go on, but you get the point.

Finally, I think it is important to emphasize the deeply theological nature of the Council as its chief legacy since the tired trope has emerged, and now seems to dominate the conversation, that the Council was purely pastoral and did not really advance any new theological construal of standard dogmas. But there were indeed dogmatic constitutions among the conciliar documents and those constitutions did introduce important developments in the theology of divine revelation and ecclesiology in particular. There were also important non-dogmatic theological developments of doctrine with regard to religious freedom, salvation for those outside of the Church, liturgy, ecumenism, and the status of non-Christian religions. Furthermore, the Council fathers put forward these theological developments precisely in order to act as a catalytic source for pastoral renewal. Therefore, the efforts of theologians such as Levering and Minerd have tremendous pastoral implications.

The pastoral aim of the Council has failed in the short term, which has given ammunition and a respectable cover to those who seek to marginalize the Council precisely because they do not agree with its theological developments. But many of the greatest councils in the Church's history have had to endure a similar tsunami of negative reaction and great controversies, some of which lasted for a century or more. Just ask St. Athanasius if he thought the post-Nicene atmosphere was irenic and open to dialogue. But as the theology developed by Nicaea eventually won the day owing to the efforts of Athanasius and others, so too today will the legacy of the theological developments of Vatican II eventually take root. And if they do, it will be because of the efforts of theologians like Levering and Minerd. May their tribe increase.

The importance of this retrieval cannot be overstated. Ross Douthat wrote recently in the *New York Times* that, like it or not, we are "trapped" by Vatican II.[3] You cannot undo it or its influence, but there is also no consensus on what it means and it seems largely dead in the water. And so there it sits on our porch, like a giant sofa too large to get in your front door but which was purchased with a no return policy. Douthat is, I think, onto something important. Namely, that right now we are stuck in neutral and unable to move forward in a positive direction or backward in a restorationist retreat.

But we cannot remain in this state forever. The Council is here to stay, and rightly so, and therefore we had better set about the business of its proper theological retrieval—with or without Rome's help.

---

3. See chapter 11.

7

The Legacy of Vatican II Is Not What George Weigel Thinks It Is

JOHN DANIEL DAVIDSON

The Federalist
October 15, 2022

GEORGE WEIGEL HAS A NEW BOOK OUT THIS WEEK about the Second Vatican Council, and for anyone familiar with Weigel's writing on the subject, his argument will come as no surprise. For those unfamiliar with Weigel's view of Vatican II, which opened sixty years ago next week, the title of his book pretty much spells it out: *To Sanctify the World: The Vital Legacy of Vatican II.*

I have not had a chance to read the book, but thankfully *The Wall Street Journal* published a long essay adaptation of it this past weekend headlined, "What Vatican II Accomplished,"[1] that outlines Weigel's thesis, which is that despite all the bad things that happened in the Church after the council, Vatican II was absolutely necessary—and its legacy, properly understood, is a vibrant and globalized Catholic Church.

I know Weigel is considered an authority on Catholic matters and a sort of elder statesman among American Catholic writers, so I take no pleasure in saying that his argument, as far as I can tell from the essay, is absolute nonsense. To begin with, he asks the wrong question. It is not, "Was Vatican II necessary?" but, "Was Vatican II *worth it*?" An honest appraisal of the current state of the Catholic Church, to say nothing of Christianity at large, should lead to a firm answer: of course not.

Set aside, for now, Weigel's historically debatable argument that the pre-Vatican II Catholic Church was somehow brittle and inef-

---

1. See chapter 21.

fectual, that "the defensive Catholicism of the Counter-Reformation, however successful a salvage operation, had run its course," and that the fragile Church of the mid-twentieth century somehow lacked "the means to express ancient and enduring truths in ways that modernity could hear." No one would argue that the Catholic Church sixty years ago was not in need of reform and renewal, or that in the face of profound societal and civilizational upheaval the Church should have been content to repose in splendid isolation.

And of course, that is not what happened. What happened was Vatican II. To assess its legacy we have only to survey the state of Catholicism today, six decades later. One need not be an expert in Church history or even a celebrated Catholic writer to know that the post-Vatican II Church is not doing well. In fact, with apologies to Weigel, it takes a certain kind of practiced insouciance to suggest that the reforms of Vatican II were an unmixed blessing, or that the many pathologies now manifesting themselves across the Catholic Church's hierarchy are not closely connected to the changes brought about in the wake of the Second Vatican Council. Arguably, in a straightforward manner, those pathologies *are* the council's legacy.

Weigel is sensible enough to acknowledge some of this in passing, noting how the postconciliar Church saw tens of thousands of priests and nuns abandon their vows and leave their rectories and convents, how liberation theology gripped the Church in Latin America, how the once-vibrant Church in western Europe withered, and how a breakdown in seminary training and priestly formation contributed to rampant clerical sexual abuse.

He also notes that "the Mass was too often dumbed down into banality, if not downright silliness," but fails to acknowledge the more disturbing truth, which is that after Vatican II the Mass was rendered ugly *on purpose* in an effort to avoid causing offense to Protestants under the theory that by accommodating the sensibilities of non-Catholics, the Catholic Church might somehow win them over—a theory that has since been thoroughly discredited. (Who ever became a Catholic because they attended a Mass that imitates an evangelical worship service? No one.)

Having duly cleared his throat, Weigel goes on to the meat of his argument: that the Second Vatican Council was never meant to rupture Catholic doctrine, only to better communicate unchanging Catholic teachings. This was necessary, he says, because after two world wars and the "cultural tsunami of the 1960s," the Catholic Church was fragile and, he implies, increasingly irrelevant. There was no way, contrary to what some Catholic traditionalists might think, that the "Catholic bastion of the mid-twentieth century could have sustained itself indefinitely."

It was both necessary and worth it, Weigel explains, because "the flourishing parts of the world Church today" are those that have embraced the true meaning of Vatican II, while those that have misunderstood and misapplied it are withering and dying off, unable to resist secular modernity.

In making his argument this way, Weigel tries to eat his cake and have it too. Every positive development in Catholicism since 1965 is because of Vatican II; every distortion or pathology is a misapplication of Vatican II. He cannot admit that perhaps there was something about the Second Vatican Council that *invited* the pathologies and ruptures, that so far from a legacy of a renewed Catholicism, the legacy of Vatican II is one of deep division within the faith and a weakening of the church's authority in the eyes of a watching world. That maybe, after all, it was not worth it.

Why is it, for example, that the truth about Jesus Christ proposed by the Catholic Church resonates most powerfully today when the Church speaks in its ancient, pre-Vatican II voice? Why is it that if you want to see a Catholic Church full of small children and young families you have to go to a Latin Mass? Why are Catholic seminaries today full of mostly traditionalist-minded young men, the sort who wear cassocks, preach with an uncompromising moral clarity against the evils of the world, and would, if Pope Francis would let them, offer the Latin Mass and Latin rites to growing numbers of parishioners hungry for them?

Weigel does not say. He does not even ask these questions. Nor does he ask why, if the legacy of the Second Vatican Council is renewal and reinvigoration, so many senior clerics—priests who would have been young men during Vatican II, who were formed in its aftermath—today are pushing for radical changes to Catholic doctrine. Why, for example, are the leaders of the Catholic Church in Ireland calling for "reforms"[2] to unchangeable church teachings on homosexual relations, women in the priesthood, and the celibacy of the clergy? Why are German and Flemish bishops now blessing same-sex unions in defiance of the Vatican?[3] Why do so many of the "listening documents" being issued by diocesan chanceries ahead of Pope Francis's forthcoming synod amount to endorsements of heresy and immorality?[4]

And why are these things happening most notably in places where the Catholic Church is shrinking, withering away like the liberalizing Protestant churches so many Catholic prelates seek to imitate? Weigel writes that "bunker Catholicism is a betrayal of the great commission," the call of Jesus Christ to go and make disciples of all nations. But the German bishops are not converting anyone to the faith by pretending that sin is not sin, or that the ancient teachings of the Church can simply be discarded in the name of "inclusiveness." If anyone is betraying the great commission, it is them.

Moreover, it is in the parishes that Weigel would likely decry for practicing "bunker Catholicism" that the future of the Catholic faith is being reared, literally, in the form of large families and young, zealous converts—the very parishes Pope Francis targeted for punishment by attempting to deprive them of the Latin Mass in his *Traditionis Custodes* issued last year. These families and converts are not being drawn to the Catholic Church and devoting themselves in ever-growing numbers to its most ancient forms of worship because the postconciliar church became more global, or because there is now a greater role for women and laity in the cele-

---

2. Synthesis of the Consultation in Ireland for the Diocesan Stage of the Universal Synod 2021–2023, https://synod.ie/wp-content/uploads/2022/08/National-Synthesis-17-50-Fri-12th-August-.pdf.

3. Philip Pullella and Charlotte Campenhout, "Defying Vatican, Flemish bishops allow blessing same-sex unions," *Reuters*, September 20, 2022, www.reuters.com/world/europe/flemish-catholic-bishops-defying-vatican-approve-blessing-same-sex-unions-2022-09-20.

4. Eric Sammons, "The Anti-Catholic Path of Synodality," *Crisis Magazine*, September 22, 2022, www.crisismagazine.com/2022/the-anti-catholic-path-of-synodality.

bration of the Mass, or because Vatican II urged Catholics to read the Bible more. They are the future of the Catholic Church,[5] and they owe the expressions of their faith more to the reforms of the sixteenth-century Council of Trent than to the twentieth-century Second Vatican Council.

If Weigel cannot see why these Catholics are drawn to the light and beauty of the ancient faith amid the wreckage of a dying civilization, then I hazard to say he has painted himself into a corner. Having convinced himself that something was profoundly wrong with the Catholic Church in the immediate post-war years, he must contend that the harsh medicine of Vatican II was the only cure. But sixty years later, it is hard not to conclude that the cure was worse than the disease, that it was in fact a slow-working poison, and that harsher medicine will yet be required to cure what ails the Church today.

5. See John Daniel Davidson, "The Latin Mass Is the Future of the Catholic Church," *The Federalist*, July 27, 2021, https://thefederalist.com/2021/07/27/the-lat in-mass-is-the-future-of-the-catholic-church.

8

"Backwardist" to the Future?[*]

FR RAYMOND J. DE SOUZA

National Catholic Register
October 11, 2022

FOR CATHOLICS TOO YOUNG TO REMEMBER THE IMME-diate postconciliar period, the sixtieth anniversary of Vatican II offers a chance to relive the past. The Church is going backwards. There is a wide consensus on that. There is disagreement over the precise historical destination.

With increasingly pointed rhetoric, Pope Francis denounces those who commit the "sin of backwardism"—a neologism he coined to characterize those he believes want to go back to before the Second Vatican Council.

The nearly ten-year pontificate of Pope Francis seems, on the other hand, to feel most comfortable in the immediate postconciliar period of the late 1960s and 1970s—before *Veritatis Splendor* (1993), the Catechism of the Catholic Church (1992), the theology of the body (1979–1984), *Familiaris Consortio* (1980) and perhaps even the entire project of St. John Paul II (elected 1978) in stabilizing the Church after a decade of turmoil.

That's the judgment of Cardinal Angelo Scola, former archbishop of both Milan and Venice, and a leading figure in the Church from the 1970s until his retirement in 2017. He published an interview book, *Betting on Freedom: My Life in the Church* in November 2021. There, the prelate of long experience and widespread esteem said that the Church is going backwards, ironically pushed by those who

---

[*] Original title: "Vatican II at 60: 'Backwardist' to the Future?" Fr Raymond J. de Souza: © 2022 EWTN News, Inc. Reprinted with permission from the *National Catholic Register* – www.ncregister.com.

incessantly clamor that the Church needs to radically move forward, lest she fall behind contemporary culture. This provokes the "backwardist" reaction that Pope Francis denounces.

"To those that think that the Church has fallen behind, I respond that we are rather going backwards, specifically to the epoch of the debates between conservatives and progressives after the Council," Cardinal Scola wrote. "I am seeing a renewed opposition, with much overexcitement, between guardians of tradition as rigidly understood and the proponents of conforming practices, but also doctrine, to worldly demands."

The Year of Faith on the fiftieth

In October 2012, Pope Benedict XVI inaugurated a "Year of Faith," marking the fiftieth anniversary of the opening of Vatican II and the twentieth anniversary of the Catechism of the Catholic Church. He noted that St. Paul VI had declared a "Year of Faith" in 1967–1968, immediately after the Council, when the ship of faith was in perilous waters.

"In some respects, [Pope Paul VI] saw this year as a 'consequence and a necessity of the postconciliar period,' fully conscious of the grave difficulties of the time, especially with regard to the profession of the true faith and its correct interpretation," wrote Benedict.

From the synods on the family and the Amazon to the current synodal process on synodality for a synodal Church, there has been no shortage of voices demanding "conforming practices, but also doctrine, to worldly demands," in Cardinal Scola's words. Hence the countervailing need, as Benedict wrote, to attend to "the profession of the true faith and its correct interpretation."

Benedict XVI would abdicate during the Year of Faith. It was a profoundly destabilizing step—all the more remarkable for having no precedent in the entire history of the Church. In retrospect, it should have been expected that such a remarkable novelty would stir up turbulent waters.

Ten years on, and the Holy Father's synodal process on synodality for a synodal Church is already threatening shipwreck, as the German Synodal Way has introduced a spirit of conformity to the world even more pronounced than in the 1970s. This time, though, there are powerful voices—like Cardinal Scola—who do not want to go back to those years. Cardinal Scola is in retirement, but his viewpoint has been forcefully articulated by large groups of bishops, including the bishops of Poland and of Scandinavia, Germany's neighbors.

Ressourcement, aggiornamento, indietrismo

The approach of Vatican II has been described using French and Italian terms: *ressourcement* and *aggiornamento*. *Ressourcement* means going back to the sources—above all Sacred Scripture, complemented by the Church Fathers and the achievements of Scholastic theology. *Aggiornamento* means "updating"—finding new ways to proclaim the Gospel in a manner suited to a post-Enlightenment world deeply scarred by two world wars and the rise of totalitarian atheism and disenchanted by secular liberalism. A healthy tension between the two always exists and errors of excess are to be found in both directions. It has ever been such, for the "kingdom of heaven is like a householder who brings out of his treasure what is new and what is old" (Matthew 13:52).

Alongside *ressourcement* and *aggiornamento*, Pope Francis has introduced another word, an Italian word of his own invention, *indietrismo*—best translated into English as "backwardism." He brandishes it against those he most frequently disparages, Catholics attached to traditional doctrine, morals, or liturgy. "This is today's problem, of many who call themselves 'traditional,'" the Holy Father said while airborne *en route* to Rome from Canada last July. "No, they are not traditional. They are *indietristi*, people who look to the past, going backward, without roots. And looking 'backward' is a sin because it does not progress with the Church."

Sin is a rather serious matter, so it is important to distinguish *indietrismo* from *ressourcement*, which characterized the theology of many greatly learned men, such as Cardinal John Henry Newman, whom Pope Francis canonized in 2019. Indeed, Newman, who died in 1890, has been called the "Father of Vatican II." Newman was not a *backwardist*, even as he immersed himself in Scripture and the patristic literature.

The Holy Father explains that instead of *backwardism* it is necessary to go upward—and downward. "Tradition is precisely the root of the inspiration to go forward in the Church," Pope Francis further explained. "And this is always vertical. And 'backwardism' is going backward; it is always closed. It is important to understand well the role of tradition, which is always open, like the roots of the tree, and the tree grows like that. . . . It is always the sap of the root that carries you forward, forward, forward. . . . So for that reason, we must think and carry forward faith and morals. As long as it is going in the direction of the roots, of the sap, it's good." "Backwardism" is horizontal and sinful; rather, one should move upward, as a tree grows, but also downward "in the direction of the roots." And "the sap carries you forward, forward." So horizontal is bad; vertical is good, but to go up it is necessary to go down in order to move forward, which trees do not do, but the Church does.

It all can appear a bit confusing. But there is one unmistakable clarity in the new papal vocabulary: One cannot go backwards.

Smoke of Satan

And yet the Church finds itself in 2022 as if it is 1972 all over again, when St. Paul VI famously spoke of the "smoke of Satan" having entered the "temple of God," obscuring the hopes of 1962 and polluting the postconciliar air. St. Paul VI made clear in his closing address to Vatican II in 1965 that *aggiornamento* "was in no way an adapting of the Church to the world, as if the latter were supposed to establish norms for the former." Too few were listening.

In a significant and welcome contribution to Vatican II's sixtieth anniversary, George Weigel has released this month *To Sanctify the World: The Vital Legacy of Vatican II*. He shows how the aspirations of 1962 were apparently dashed by 1972, as a Church meant to be revitalized with new evangelical energy instead consumed herself with internecine debates about whether divine Revelation was still valid. Could God still be known and proclaimed to the world? And if so, would that be good for the world?

Weigel quotes Paul VI's esteemed and close friend Jacques Maritain, who saw in the immediate aftermath of Vatican II "a kind of kneeling before the world," a "complete temporalization of Christianity," in which "there is no kingdom of God distinct from the world."

"By the early 1970s," Weigel writes, "the Church appeared to be coming apart at the seams—thanks to vast defections from the priesthood and consecrated religious life, open disdain for papal teaching among theologians and some bishops, and a rapid dissolution of Catholic practice at the grassroots."

"Maritain, that great influence on the Second Vatican Council and defender of its achievements," adds Weigel, "had presciently discerned a vast, postconciliar confusion that was impeding the evangelical springtime for which John XXIII, Paul VI, and Maritain himself had hoped."

Clearing the air

In Weigel's telling, the nadir of 1972 was definitively answered by 1992 and the Catechism, the joint project of John Paul and Benedict, representative of a forty-year project, 1972–2012, to give Vatican II an authoritative and authentic interpretation. The abdication of 2013 then opened the door for backsliding under Pope Francis to the early 1970s, even as he inveighs against *backwardism*.

The synodal process of the synod on synodality for a synodal Church may well deliver the Church—one year from now and ten years after the conclusion of Benedict's Year of Faith—backwards fifty years to the early 1970s.

Yet those who desire to drag the Church back to 1972 will have to contend with the forty years from 1972 to 2012, from St. Paul VI's *Evangelii Nuntiandi* to Benedict's trilogy of biblical theology, *Jesus of Nazareth*. Those who desire in 2022 to go back to 1972 have to contend with the colossus of 1992, the Catechism and the entire John Paul-Benedict project of which it was the capstone.

The ship of faith is being steered back to the rough waters of 1972. But this time she goes back with a great deal more ballast in the boat.

On the sixtieth anniversary of Vatican II, it may seem like the tenth anniversary again. But only in part, not in whole, and this time with many more discernible reasons for hope.

The year ahead will reveal who the true *backwardists* are.

9

Paul VI Did Not Exist:
A "Nostalgic" Response to George Weigel

GREGORY DIPIPPO

OnePeterFive
October 24, 2022

When Vatican II turned forty

Twenty years ago, a week before the fortieth anniversary of the opening of Vatican II, Mr George Weigel, a great admirer of that assembly, wrote an assessment of it for, of all publications, the *National Catholic Reporter*.[1] The basic thrust of his column is simple: a reading of Vatican II as a power struggle within the Church is incorrect. He does not deny that the Church has collectively "got(ten) Vatican II wrong" in many ways, and did so "by thinking of it chiefly in terms of church politics." But in "the council's masterwork," *Lumen Gentium*, we see that "the universal call to holiness, not the struggle for ecclesiastical power, was the central motif of Vatican II." This is both true and a good thing to say, especially in a publication so deeply invested in reading Vatican II and its aftermath as a series of power struggles: of bishops against an overcentralized papacy and curia; of heretical theologians against bishops; and ultimately, of Modern Man™ against the Faith once delivered to the Saints.

But twenty years ago, Mr Weigel was still able to entertain some doubts as to the ultimate fate of Vatican II in the Church's life, and he goes on to say:

> I've been much struck recently by the question of whether, in the mid-third millennium, Vatican II will be remembered as another

---

1. See "Grateful for Vatican II, even when we 'get it wrong,'" *NCR Online*, October 4, 2002, www.natcath.org/NCR_Online/archives/100402/100402j.htm.

Lateran V or another Trent. Lateran V was a reforming council that failed; Trent was a reforming council whose success defined Catholic life for almost four centuries. Lateran V's failure was one cause of the fracture of Western Christianity in the Reformation— and thus of the wars of religion, the rise of the modern state, and the gradual erosion of Christian culture in Europe. Getting it wrong, in this business of conciliar reform, can carry high costs.

With all due respect, this question was put incorrectly. By its fortieth anniversary, Vatican II was already neither another Lateran V nor another Trent.

Trent began in 1545, which puts its fortieth anniversary in 1585. By that point, the Church had already made huge strides in implementing the reforms which it had ordered, and the movement to continue doing so was gaining strength every day, with the strong leadership and support of the Papacy. The spread of Protestantism had been checked in much of Europe, and reversed in some places; the evangelization of the New World was proceeding apace. New religious orders such as the Jesuits and Oratorians were thriving and spreading, and inspiring the older ones to highly successful reforms. The model of Counter-Reformation bishops, St Charles Borromeo, was still alive, and a leading figure in the implementation of the Council's decrees.

It hardly needs saying that forty years out from Vatican II, the Church was not thriving as it was in 1585.

On the other hand, the fortieth anniversary of Lateran V occurred in 1552… smack in the middle of the Council of Trent. Forty years after Lateran V had failed so spectacularly to bring about any of the reform that the Church so desperately needed (and by so failing, had helped to trigger the Reformation), the Church did not content itself with monomaniacal repetition of the catchphrase, "You have to accept Lateran V!," while ignoring the fact that everything was burning down around it. Rather, it recognized that its previous feint at reform had failed catastrophically, and set about at Trent to do well what it had done badly at Lateran V.

It hardly needs saying that forty years out from Vatican II, the Church wasn't doing this either.

The truest parallel with Vatican II to be found among the ecumenical councils is that of Constance (1414–1418), the highwater mark of the Conciliarist movement, which taught that the ecumenical council as an institution is superior in authority to the Pope (i.e., a power-struggle: so ironic...).[2] A wave of enthusiasm for something new, something which everyone hopes will bring great benefit to the Church, is quickly followed by a sudden and almost inexplicable dissipation of that enthusiasm. Just as the bishops who attended Constance did not bother to attend the next council which they themselves had called for, the bishops who wrote (with their *periti*) and approved the documents of Vatican II seemed afterwards to care little or nothing for what they had written.

Weigel himself acknowledges as much in the same column:

> I never seriously read the texts of Vatican II until the mid-1970s, despite eight years in high school and college seminary and two years of graduate studies in theology. I don't think I was alone in this. [*No, he most certainly wasn't.*] In those days, one read about the council ... (but) one didn't wrestle with the texts of the council itself.

I have yet to see a convincing explanation of why I or anyone else should show an enthusiasm for the texts of Vatican II which their own authors never showed, but Mr Weigel's enthusiasm for them, at any rate, knows no abatement.

When Vatican II turned fifty

Ten years after the aforementioned column, it was time to commemorate the council's golden anniversary; the venue changed to an incommensurably more Catholic publication, *First Things*, and so did the tack.[3] In a very brief article, he notes (how could one not?) that "Vatican II is sometimes imagined to be an example of ecclesiastical parthenogenesis: the Council just happened, absent significant antecedents, in a decisive rupture with the past." But this

---

2. See Gregory DiPippo, "Another Lesson from a Conciliar Failure," *New Liturgical Movement*, September 16, 2021, www.newliturgicalmovement.org/2021/09/another-lesson-from-conciliar-failure.html.

3. "Vatican II's Golden Anniversary," *First Things* online, October 10, 2012, www.firstthings.com/web-exclusives/2012/10/vatican-iis-golden-anniversary.

imagining is incorrect: Popes since Leo XIII, he tells us, had been coming to grips with modernity, and Vatican II was, or was supposed to be, the culmination of this engagement.

However, the future reception of Vatican II is no longer to be understood by looking at any previous council:

> [It] was like no other ecumenical Council in history, in that it did not provide authoritative keys for its own interpretation: the Council Fathers wrote no creed, condemned no heresy, legislated no new canons, defined no dogmas. Thus the decade and a half after the Council ended on December 8, 1965, was a bit of a free-for-all, as varying interpretations of the Council (including appeals to an amorphous "spirit of Vatican II" that seems to have more in common with low-church Protestantism than with Catholicism) contended with each other in what amounted to an ecclesiastical civil war.

Just "a bit of a free-for-all," he writes, like a British general of a *sang* particularly *froid* describing the Second World War. (Fifty years from the opening of Lateran V, by the way, brings us to the opening of the third and final session of Trent; fifty years from the opening of Trent, and Rome is getting ready to celebrate its second Jubilee of the Counter-Reformation.) Why the free-for-all? Because the Council "did not provide authoritative keys for its own interpretation." Is it cynical to ask whether this was really a wise procedure for a body whose very *raison d'être* is to bring much needed clarity to the Church?

Never fear. The free-for-all is over, because

> Providence raised up two men of genius, John Paul II and Benedict XVI ... to give Vatican II an authoritative interpretation (and) the truth about the Council. ... Vatican II did not displace the Church's tradition. Vatican II did not create do-it-yourself-Catholicism.

What a relief.

When Vatican II turned sixty

Now, another ten years have passed, and any doubts Mr Weigel might once have entertained about the place of Vatican II in the Church's future life have evaporated as thoroughly as... well, as thoroughly as the enthusiasm of the world's bishops for Vatican II did after December 8, 1965. In a recent column for the *Wall Street Journal*, he brands it "the most important Catholic event in half a millennium." From the Council's own starting date, that brings us back to 1462, fifty years before Lateran V began; from our present year, back to 1522, five years after Lateran V ended and the Protestant Reformation began. Were it not for the previous assurance that Vatican II is like no other council, and historical parallelism thus dismissed, some might find this worrisome.

It is no longer a question of whether Vatican II will be seen in the future as a successful council like Trent or a failed one like Lateran V. The title of the column, published in advance of a book on the subject released one week before the anniversary, is simply "What Vatican II Accomplished."[4] As in "Mission Accomplished"?

What a relief.

The subheader, however, does not briefly summarize these achievements, but like the column itself, brings in the boogeymen, assuring us that "progressives and nostalgic traditionalists" have misunderstood the Council. Vatican II turns out to be as singularly unlucky in its application as socialism, communism, and the other disgusting -isms of the twentieth century which it so conspicuously failed to condemn. "If only we had REAL socialism..."

If the job of a subheader is to summarize a column, John Daniel Davidson of *The Federalist* wrote a sentence about this column that would have served the purpose far better: "Every positive development in Catholicism since 1965 is because of Vatican II; every distortion or pathology is a misapplication of Vatican II."[5]

For we are assured by Weigel that

> from his historical studies and pastoral experience, John XXIII knew that the defensive Catholicism of the Counter-Reformation, however successful a salvage operation, had run its course. It was time to raze the bastions that Catholicism had erected and turn its robust institutions into platforms for evangelization and mission in order to engage a deeply troubled modern world.

4. See chapter 21.
5. See chapter 7.

And in brief, despite whatever difficulties the Church may be undergoing right now, or may have been undergoing for the last several decades, this is what the Council has purportedly achieved.

The Pope of the Council

This is one of nineteen mentions of Pope John by name, in a column of just under 2100 words, which is an average of about one every 110 words. The unknowing reader might be forgiven for getting the impression that the Council itself was actually his work and faithful to his intentions. But Weigel himself knows this to be untrue, and carefully describes those intentions in the conditional mood (emphasis added):

> In his opening address to Vatican II, John XXIII suggested how ecclesiastical renewal *would* take place.... the Church *would* develop the means to express ancient and enduring truths in ways that modernity could hear ... his hope that Vatican II *would* be a "new Pentecost."

By this sleight of hand, the Pope who called Vatican II becomes something like a large, disembodied head, floating above the floor and loudly proclaiming, "I! AM!! JOHN!!! The great and powerful!" Wicked, nostalgic traditionalists, get away from that curtain...

Missing from this and so many other discourses about the reception of the Council and its purported achievements is Paul VI, the Pope in whose reign all of the Council's documents were promulgated, and who, by his action and inaction over the years that followed it, "implemented" it in ways that thoroughly betrayed those documents and the intentions of Pope John. Even twenty years ago, when the future reception of Vatican II was still a matter of uncertainty, he merited from Weigel no more than a passing mention in reference to his 1965 visit to the U.N. (an institution which constitutes one of the most conspicuous among Modern Man™'s great and ghastly political failures). By the fiftieth anniversary, he had been thrown down the memory hole. Did the decade and a half which Mr Weigel describes as a "bit of a free-for-all" after the end of Vatican II happen to coincide with anything in particular?

Get away from that curtain!

Now, at the sixtieth anniversary, in telling us "What Vatican II

Accomplished," Mr Weigel gives us not a hint of who specifically steered it towards its accomplishments. We must not think of Vatican II as an instance of "ecclesiastical parthenogenesis," but we are left free to think of its accomplishments as products of spontaneous generation, without father, without mother, and without genealogy.

To rehearse these "achievements" in detail would be as unbearably tedious for you to read as it would be for me to write. I will therefore limit myself to commenting on the first which Mr Weigel enumerates, one which happily coincides with my own area of interest and, such as it is, expertise.

He tells us that "After Vatican II, Catholics worshiped in their own languages, rather than in Latin." But he does not tell us that the general postconciliar abandonment of Latin happened in direct contradiction of the Apostolic Constitution *Veterum Sapientia*, which John XXIII promulgated eight months before Vatican II: an "achievement," in Weigel's presentation, "without father."

He does not tell us that the all-vernacular liturgy was brought about in direct contradiction to *Sacrosanctum Concilium*, the Council's Constitution on the Sacred Liturgy, which states that the use of Latin was to be preserved in the liturgy.

"Without mother."

He does not tell us that when a Sicilian bishop urged the Council Fathers to be cautious about accepting liturgical use of the vernacular, lest a partial permission turn into a Mass with no Latin at all, there was a brief pause, followed by an explosion of laughter, so absurd did the very idea seem to them.

He does not tell us that the Council's other fifteen documents contain only one brief mention of Latin, precisely because it was taken for granted that *Veterum Sapientia* had fully dealt with the subject, and there was no need to say any more. Nor indeed could any of them have imagined that any Pope would so cavalierly ignore such an act of his predecessor.

On November 26, 1969, at the last general audience before the promulgation of the Novus Ordo, Paul VI informed the Church that although Latin would no longer be the principal language of the Mass, it would "remain as the means of teaching in ecclesiastical studies and as the key to the patrimony of our religious, historical and human culture. If possible, it will reflourish in splendor." Mr Weigel does not tell us that that is exactly what John XXIII ordered in *Veterum Sapientia*, or that *none of that happened either.*

"Without genealogy."

As a segue, he tells us that the Council "urged Catholics to become more biblically literate." He does not tell us that the Holy See under Paul VI stayed mostly silent as Catholic Biblical scholars introduced all the most fatuous excesses of modern Biblical scholarship into Catholic seminaries and schools, from which they slithered down into sermons and catechism classes. Nor are we told that the revised lectionary of the postconciliar Mass routinely censors and violently misrepresents the word of God. Vatican II's Dogmatic Constitution on Divine Revelation *Dei Verbum* says that "with maternal concern, the Church sees to it that suitable and correct translations are made into different languages," but we are not told that the official translation used for the Biblical readings at Mass in the United States is the "colorless, odorless, gaseous paraphrase"[6] known as the New American Bible, nor that it is full of the most gruesome errors.

Sad tales of this sort can be and have been told repeatedly about every aspect of the Church's life over the last sixty years, and they all amount to pretty much the same thing.

The Church lives as it lives now very largely because Paul VI rejected and did not fulfill the will of the Second Vatican Council.

Twenty years ago, Weigel's rhetorical combination of *suppressio veri* and *suggestio falsi* did perhaps serve a legitimate function, not as history or theology, but as propaganda.[7] It encouraged us to believe in one possible understanding of Vatican II, of how it ought

---

6. The phrase is from Anthony Esolen, "A Bumping Boxcar Language," *First Things*, June 2011, online at www.firstthings.com/article/2011/06/a-bumping-boxcar -language.

7. I would not, of course, say this on the basis of a single column, or three columns. Omitting mention of Paul VI or downplaying him has been a leitmotif of Mr Weigel's writings about Vatican II and its reception for some time. We have the assertion that St John XXIII was ideologically hijacked, in which we are told that "it took the Church more than twenty years to grasp the full meaning of *Gaudet Mater Ecclesia*," the opening speech which he delivered at Vatican II, without mentioning

to have been implemented, and the prior implementation of it corrected. Whatever the flaws of this understanding may have been, it was certainly better than Paul VI's. As a priest friend of mine put it to me in mid-2013, "the background radiation (in the Church) was dying down." St John Paul II and Benedict XVI unquestionably deserve a great deal of the credit for that. Ten years ago, the last full year of Benedict's reign, it was fully plausible that their far healthier version of Vatican II might prevail, and the worst excesses of the Paul VI years would simply fade into the past and be gently, deservedly forgotten.

Revolution reborn

But this was before the election of Francis, a man of a very different spirit, who has canonized John XXIII, Paul VI, and John Paul II, but revived the ghost of only one of them. The first Pope to never serve

who was Pope for most of those twenty years, and responsible for obscuring its meaning. (Is it cynical to ask if the Pope should be making speeches that take more than twenty years to understand?) We have the assertion that the Berlin Wall fell because once John Paul II became Pope, Eastern Europeans knew "that 'Rome' now had their backs (as it hadn't in the 1970s)," without mentioning who was Pope during the 1970s, when it didn't have their backs. (Mr Weigel usually assigns most of the blame for the obscene moral failure of Ostpolitik to Paul VI's Secretary of State, Card. Agostino Casaroli.) We are told that "The War of the Conciliar Succession" has been going on since the '60s, without being told whose failure to rein in the heresies festering in every corner of the Church made such a war first possible, and then necessary. In his 2019 book *The Irony of Modern Catholic History*, "Vatican II" is mentioned over 300 times by name, and over 250 times as "the Council"; Paul VI, who promulgated all of its documents, is mentioned just over eighty times; John XXIII, who promulgated none of them, over one hundred times, John Paul II nearly 280. In *Evangelical Catholicism* (2013), "Vatican II" is mentioned over 250 times by name, and 145 times as "the Council"; Paul VI 15 times; John XXIII, only 9 times, John Paul II, over 200. And in a recent podcast about his new book on Vatican II, we learn from Mr Weigel that "a lot of mistakes were made in implementing the Council" (6:40), in the passive-voice-of-unattributed-responsibility. Probably not by anybody in particular... (Sources of the above claims: https://denvercatholic.org/the-ideological-hijacking-of-pope-st-john-xxiii/; https://cathstan.org/voices/george-weigel/the-catholic-difference-why-did-the-wall-fall-30-years-ago; www.firstthings.com/web-exclusives/2022/07/the-war-of-the-conciliar-succession-continued; www.nationalreview.com/podcasts/the-bookmonger/episode-424-to-sanctify-the-world-by-george-weigel).

as a priest in the Church as it was before the Montinian revolution is committed to that revolution as Papa Montini himself never was. That brings with it a commitment to a violent, revolutionary interpretation of Vatican II, and all that goes with it: the power struggles which Weigel rejected twenty years ago, the "ecclesiastical parthenogenesis" which he rejected ten years ago, and many other interpretations of Vatican II which he deems inauthentic.

I would be utterly remiss were I not to say that Catholics ought to be sincerely grateful to Mr Weigel for speaking out against this as he has in recent times. Despite no evident fondness for the traditional Roman liturgy, he rightly decried the "Liberal Authoritarianism" of *Traditionis Custodes*, and rightly branded it "theologically incoherent, pastorally divisive, unnecessary, cruel—and a sorry example of the liberal bullying that has become all too familiar in Rome recently." When the responses to the so-called dubia about TC followed, he pointed out the absurdity of "Undercutting Vatican II to Defend Vatican II" by issuing orders to the bishops wholly contrary to the spirit of *Lumen Gentium*. He has repeatedly denounced the *de facto* revival of Paul VI's Ostpolitik in the Vatican's current dealings with the single most murderous organization in human history, the Chinese Communist Party. He has called the recent developments in the Pontifical Academy for Life a second assassination attempt against John Paul II. And this is all to the good.

As important as these matters are, however, they do not lie at the heart of the Vatican II problem.

Ten years ago, Mr Weigel told us that "Providence raised up John Paul II and Benedict XVI . . . to give Vatican II an authoritative interpretation." "Authoritative" according to whom? According to Mr Weigel himself? By all means. But according to Francis, who has set out to destroy some of their crucial achievements: John Paul's in the field of sexual ethics, Benedict's in liturgy, and of both of them on the question of moral relativism? *Not by any means*, and in this dispute, it is Francis, not Weigel, who counts.

And there is simply no reason why Vatican II should not *always* be plagued with this problem, pushed aside by acts of papal power, and "interpreted" to mean whatever that power wants it to mean, just as Paul VI did. It is being so plagued at this very moment.

The Third Vatican Council

In his 1999 biography of St John Paul II, *Witness to Hope*, Weigel writes that

> Twenty years after (Vatican II) had closed . . . (a) 'progressive' party in the Church, thinking Vatican II rather old hat, was busy imagining a Vatican III that would complete the rout of traditional Catholicism which it somehow thought to be John XXIII's intention in summoning the Council.

That party is no longer "busy imagining"; it is busy putting its imaginings into practice. Cardinal Mario Grech, secretary general of the Synod of Bishops, and stage manager of the current Pope's pet project, the Synod on Synodultery, somehow managed to be very frank about the matter during a recent lecture of almost Teilhardian unintelligibility.

> The current synodal process is a "mature fruit of Vatican II" and shows how "a correct reception of the Council's ecclesiology is activating such fruitful processes as to open up *scenarios that not even the Council had imagined* and in which the action of the Spirit that guides the Church is made manifest."[8]

Earlier today (as I write), a Mass was celebrated to commemorate the beginning of the most recent ecumenical council in the very place where it began sixty years ago. Sitting just a few steps away from St Peter's tomb, the Holy Father, always ready with an unkind word for his children, once again trotted out his new favorite insult for traditionalists. This is an Italian word of his own devising, "*indietristi*," which is as clumsy in the mouth as it is in the mind, but easier to say in English, "backwardists." "Both progressivism, which lines up behind the world, and traditionalism, or 'backwardism,' that longs for a bygone world, are not evidence of love, but of faithlessness," say the pope.

Wonder no longer if the Listening Church will ever extend its listening to "backwardists." Wonder instead how many progressives heard that and said to themselves, "Wait, aren't we in charge now?

---

8. See "Cardinal Grech: Synodal process is mature fruit of Vatican II," *Vatican News*, October 5, 2022, www.vaticannews.va/en/vatican-city/news/2022-10/cardinal -grech-synodal-process-is-mature-fruit-of-vatican-ii.html.

Didn't he PUT us in charge?" As another papal biographer, Henry Sire, explained a few years ago, this is the very essence of Peronism, and Peronism is the essence of Francis. You may not be interested in power, but power is extremely interested in you.

But alas, alas for the backwardists, those who are always looking backwards to the 1970s, when the bastions of the Counter-Reformation had indeed been razed, and the world flooded into the Church, bringing chaos and destruction with it, and the words of the most recent ecumenical council lay safely buried and undigested in the stomach of its spirit. Alas also for the nostalgic, those who are always looking back to the aughts of this century, when the bastions of John Paul and Benedict had not yet been razed, and it was still possible to imagine, at least sometimes, a Church in which Paul VI did not exist.

10

Slouching from Slogan to Slogan[*]

MICHAEL BRENDAN DOUGHERTY

National Review
October 12, 2022

YEARS AGO, DURING A VERY BRIEF MEETING AT NEW York University with the eminent English conservative Roger Scruton, I shared with him—an Anglican by tradition—my reservations about the Second Vatican Council and my interest in the old liturgy. He had no reservation in his analysis. He said more or less that the Catholic Church had "joined in the spirit of self-hatred and suicide" that pervaded the West in the 1960s.

My reservations turned into doubts and real problems. They were echoed at the very top. "The truth is that the Vatican Council II itself has not defined any dogma and has consciously wanted to express itself in a more modest range, merely as a pastoral Council," Pope Benedict XVI would explain. "However, many interpret it as almost a super-dogma that takes away everything else."

Sixty years ago, Evelyn Waugh wrote in *National Review* about his expectations and reservations regarding the Second Vatican Council, just then beginning. It is hard now to recall that a giddy ecumenical hope was one of the council's guiding spirits. Protestant and Orthodox theologians were invited to witness the council. Waugh poured a bucket of ice on this hope:

> There is no possibility of the Church's modifying her defined doctrines to attract those to whom they are repugnant. The Orthodox Churches of the East, with whom the doctrinal differences are small and technical, are more hostile to Rome than are the Protestants. To them the sack and occupation of Constantinople for the

---

[*] Original title: "60 Years Since Vatican II."

first half of the thirteenth century—an event which does not bulk large in the historical conspectus of the West—is as lively and bitter a memory as is Hitler's persecution to the Jews. Miracles are possible; it is presumptuous to expect them; only a miracle can reconcile the East with Rome.

This is true. The Vatican Council could not satisfy doctrinal Protestants still committed to the fundamentals of the Reformation, because the church would not—and I would hold could not—explicitly repudiate the doctrines of the Mass, the sacerdotal priesthood, her Marian dogmas, or papal supremacy. And, the church could not satisfy liberal Protestants who objected to the church's continued intransigence on moral and sacramental issues and its hierarchical nature. Rome was against artificial birth control, divorce, and homosexuality.[1]

What are the fruits of Vatican II? For those who pay very close attention to gossip about the Roman curia, the question is a hilarious and homophobic joke that answers itself.

But it's worth recalling that Vatican II was billed at the time as a second Pentecost by its greatest enthusiasts. And even now, theologians describe it by borrowing the language of French communist Alain Baidou. Vatican II was an "Event"[2]—a rupture in being that brings into light new truths and new paradigms for self-understanding. For Baidou, the great event was the Chinese Cultural Revolution, and the only true philosopher was Mao Zedong. For modernist Catholics, Vatican II was the one true event, one that transformed Catholicism as it had been understood and practiced for centuries into Pharisaism and then tried to redirect Christian energies into deconstructing the old church. That is, until the subsequent popes (John Paul II, Benedict XVI) betrayed their revolution by insisting on doctrinal continuity.

Obviously, the greatest legacy of the council was liturgical. Its

1. See Graham A. Duncan, "A Protestant perspective on Vatican II & 50 years: An engagement with dissent," *HTS Theological Studies* 69.1 (Jan. 2013), www.scielo.org.za/scielo.php?script=sci_arttext&pid=S0259-94222013000100025.

2. See Michael Brendan Dougherty, "Roma Locuta Est, Deal With It," *National Review*, October 28, 2019, www.nationalreview.com/2019/10/roma-locuta-est-deal-with-it.

document on the liturgy seems to call for some continuity, including the retainment of Latin and Gregorian chant. But footnotes throughout envision a top-to-bottom overhaul of every physical and verbal aspect of Catholic worship, which is what we got. Some enthusiasts view this as renewal; I view it as the greatest spasm of iconoclasm in the history of Christendom.

But again, Pope Benedict XVI cut to the core problem of a new liturgy that was created by committee and imposed universally: It tended toward a church ruled by experts and a community "only celebrating itself":

> But the fact that [the liturgy] was presented as a new structure, set up against what had been formed in the course of history and was now prohibited, and that the liturgy was made to appear in some ways no longer as a living process but as a product of specialized knowledge and juridical competence, has brought with it some extremely serious damages for us.
>
> In this way, in fact, the impression has arisen that the liturgy is "made," that it is not something that exists before us, something "given," but that it depends on our decisions. It follows as a consequence that this decision-making capacity is not recognized only in specialists or in a central authority, but that, in the final analysis, each "community" wants to give itself its own liturgy. But when the liturgy is something each one makes by himself, then it no longer gives us what is its true quality: encounter with the mystery which is not our product but our origin and the wellspring of our life.

And this leads me to the other astounding feature of the post–Vatican II church: the incredible proliferation of pseudo-theological jargon and relative absence of talk about Christ, and what He asks of us. The modern liturgy, it was said endlessly, has more of a "horizontal" emphasis than a "vertical" one. What did any of that mean? Was it a comment about transcendence versus communitarianism? It suggested that Catholics at Mass were now more like children on a playdate, rather than worshippers of a living God.

Catholic theologians and bishops have been turned into sponges, soaked in metaphors that have no precise theological content but which retain an acid-wash quality, an iconoclasm aimed at a

Church and a theology of the past that is half understood, at best. So modernists such as Hans Küng could say that Vatican II promoted a "*communio* model of the church" over and against an "absolutist pyramidal model."

None of this was meant with any real conviction. It was an ad hoc theology developed for the sole purpose of legitimating dissent on moral issues touching sexuality. In Küng's model, if the pew sitters could be shown to not be following this teaching, then the teaching itself should be jettisoned. But this has lately been junked for more papal primacy, because the current pope is seen as more progressive than some of the pew sitters.

The Church has thus proceeded from slogan to slogan, as if theological reflection or—more ominously—the development of doctrine were mere rumination on the latest sets of buzzwords, usually coming from bishops or the pope. The People of God in transit, the listening Church, the New Evangelization, the field hospital. The synodal Church. Catholics used to be known by their distinctive devotional life—prayers to the saints, rosaries, abstaining from meat on Fridays. Now, devoted Catholics spend their time reading papal encyclicals and mastering this pseudo-theological jargon.

Blah blah blah. Can we ever talk about God, sin, redemption, Our Lord and Our Lady? Heaven and hell? Oddly, it was Mike Judge who managed to capture and satirize the post-Vatican II church. Beavis turns to the crucifix and says, "I'm willing to do whatever it takes."[3] The priest then extinguishes his nascent faith by drowning it with modern Catholic logorrhea. Beavis then does what most American Catholics do; he leaves.

3. See "Beavis visits a Roman Catholic Church" (S1 E10), October 9, 2022, https://youtu.be/oUeShUhnZnk.

11

How Catholics Became Prisoners of Vatican II [*]

ROSS DOUTHAT

New York Times
October 12, 2022

THE SECOND VATICAN COUNCIL, THE GREAT REVOLU-
tion in the life of the modern Catholic Church, opened sixty years
ago this week in Rome. So much of that 1960s-era world has passed
away, but the council is still with us; indeed for a divided church its
still-unfolding consequences cannot be escaped.

For a long time this would have been a liberal claim. In the wars
within Catholicism that followed the council, the conservatives
interpreted Vatican II as a discrete and limited event—a particular
set of documents that contained various shifts and evolutions (on
religious liberty and Catholic-Jewish relations especially) and
opened the door to a revised, vernacular version of the Mass. For
the liberals, though, these specifics were just the starting place:
There was also a "spirit" of the council, similar to the Holy Spirit in
its operation, that was supposed to guide the church into further
transformations, perpetual reform.

The liberal interpretation dominated Catholic life in the 1960s
and 1970s, when Vatican II was invoked to justify an ever-wider
array of changes—to the church's liturgy and calendar and prayers,
to lay customs and clerical dress, to church architecture and sacred
music, to Catholic moral discipline. Then the conservative interpretation took hold in Rome with the election of John Paul II, who
issued a flotilla of documents intended to establish an authoritative

reading of Vatican II, to rein in the more radical experiments and alterations, to prove that Catholicism before the 1960s and Catholicism afterward were still the same tradition.

Now in the years of Pope Francis, the liberal interpretation has returned—not just in the reopening of moral and theological debates, the establishment of a permanent listening-session style of church governance, but also in the attempt to once again suppress the older Catholic rites, the traditional Latin liturgy as it existed before Vatican II.

The Francis era has not restored the youthful vigor that progressive Catholicism once enjoyed, but it has vindicated part of the liberal vision. Through his governance and indeed through his mere existence, this liberal pope has proved that the Second Vatican Council cannot be simply reduced to a single settled interpretation, or have its work somehow deemed finished, the period of experimentation ended and synthesis restored.

Instead, the council poses a continuing challenge, it creates intractable-seeming divisions, and it leaves contemporary Catholicism facing a set of problems and dilemmas that Providence has not yet seen fit to resolve.

Here are three statements to encapsulate the problems and dilemmas. First, *the council was necessary.* Maybe not in the exact form it took, an ecumenical council summoning all the bishops from around the world, but in the sense that the church of 1962 needed significant adaptations, significant rethinking and reform. These adaptations needed to be backward-looking: The death of throne-and-altar politics, the rise of modern liberalism and the horror of the Holocaust all required fuller responses from the church. And they also needed to be forward-looking, in the sense that Catholicism in the early 1960s had only just begun to reckon with globalization and decolonization, with the information age and the social revolutions touched off by the invention of the contraceptive pill.

Tradition has always depended on reinvention, changing to remain the same, but Vatican II was called at a moment when the need for such change was about to become particularly acute.

But just because a moment calls for reinvention doesn't mean that a specific set of reinventions will succeed, and we now have decades of data to justify a second encapsulating statement: *The council was a failure.*

This isn't a truculent or reactionary analysis. The Second Vatican Council failed on the terms its own supporters set. It was supposed to make the church more dynamic, more attractive to modern people, more evangelistic, less closed off and stale and self-referential. It did none of these things. The church declined everywhere in the developed world after Vatican II, under conservative and liberal popes alike—but the decline was swiftest where the council's influence was strongest.

The new liturgy was supposed to make the faithful more engaged with the Mass; instead, the faithful began sleeping in on Sunday and giving up Catholicism for Lent. The church lost much of Europe to secularism and much of Latin America[1] to Pentecostalism—very different contexts and challengers, yet strikingly similar results.

And if anything, post-1960s Catholicism became *more* inward-looking than before, more consumed with its endless right-versus-left battles, and to the extent it engaged with the secular world, it was in paltry imitation—via middling guitar music or political theories that were just dressed-up versions of left-wing or right-wing partisanship or ugly modern churches that were outdated ten years after they were built and empty soon thereafter.

There is no clever rationalization, no intellectual schematic, no sententious Vatican propaganda—a typical recent document refers to "the life-giving sustenance provided by the council," as though it were the Eucharist itself—that can evade this cold reality.

But neither can anyone evade the third reality: *The council cannot be undone.*

By this I don't mean that the Mass can never return to Latin or that various manifestations of postconciliar Catholicism are inevitable and eternal or that cardinals in the twenty-third century will still be issuing Soviet-style praise for the council and its works.

1. See David Masci, "Why has Pentecostalism grown so dramatically in Latin America?," *Pew Research Center*, November 14, 2014, www.pewresearch.org/fact-tank/2014/11/14/why-has-pentecostalism-grown-so-dramatically-in-latin-america.

I just mean that there is no simple path back. Not back to the style of papal authority that both John Paul II and Francis have tried to exercise—the former to restore tradition, the latter to suppress it—only to find themselves frustrated by the ungovernability of the modern church. Not to the kind of thick inherited Catholic cultures that still existed down to the middle of the twentieth century, and whose subsequent unraveling, while inevitable to some extent, was clearly accelerated by the church's own internal iconoclasm. Not to the moral and doctrinal synthesis, stamped with the promise of infallibility and consistency, that the church's conservatives have spent the last two generations insisting still exists, but that in the Francis era has proved so unstable that those same conservatives have ended up feuding with the pope himself.

The work of the French historian Guillaume Cuchet, who has studied Vatican II's impact on his once deeply Catholic nation, suggests that it was the scale and speed of the council's reforms, as much as any particular substance, that shattered Catholic loyalty and hastened the church's decline.[2] Even if the council's changes did not officially alter doctrine, to rewrite and renovate so many prayers and practices inevitably made ordinary Catholics wonder why an authority that suddenly declared itself to have been misguided across so many different fronts could still be trusted to speak on behalf of Jesus Christ himself.

After such a shock, what kind of synthesis or restoration is possible? Today all Catholics find themselves living with this question, because every one of the church's factions is in tension with some version of church authority. Traditionalists are in tension with the Vatican's official policies, progressives with its traditional teachings, conservatives with the liberalizing style of Pope Francis, the pope himself with the conservative emphasis of his immediate predecessors. In this sense, all of us are the children of Vatican II, even if we critique or lament the council—or perhaps never more so than when we do.

Here, again, the liberals have a point. The most traditionalist Catholics are stamped by what began in 1962 as surely as this anti-

2. See chapter 17.

traditionalist pope, and the merely conservative—such as, well, myself—are often in the position described by Peter Hitchens, writing about the European high culture shattered by World War I: We may admire the lost world's intensity and rigors, but "none of us, now, could bear to return to it even if we were offered the chance."[3]

But this point does not vindicate the council, let alone the ever-evolving liberal interpretation of its spirit. The church has to live with Vatican II, wrestle with it, somehow resolve the contradictions it bequeathed us, not because it was a triumph but precisely because it wasn't: Failure casts a longer and more enduring shadow, sometimes, than success.

You begin from where you are. The lines of healing run along the lines of fracture, the wounds remain after the resurrection, and even the Catholicism that arrives, not today but someday, at a true *After Vatican II* will still be marked by the unnecessary breakages created by its attempt at a necessary reform.

3. Peter Hitchens, "The turn of the year is no cause for optimism," *UnHerd*, December 31, 2019, https://unherd.com/2019/12/the-world-we-lost-will-never-return.

12

How Vatican II Failed Catholics —and Catholicism*

ROSS DOUTHAT

New York Times
November 4, 2022

A COUPLE OF YEARS AGO AT A PARTY, I FELL INTO A conversation with a friendly older gentleman, an Irish American of the Baby Boom generation and the greater tristate area. At some point, the discussion turned to family life and the challenges of dragging complaining kids to church, and I said something in passing about the Sunday Obligation, meaning the requirement laid on Catholics to attend Mass on pain of serious sin.

He looked at me with a friendly sort of mystification. "Oh," he said, "but you know the church got rid of that after Vatican II?"

I didn't really argue with him. Catholicism was deep in his bones, he had been educated by nuns once upon a time, who was I to tell him what his faith really teaches?

But I think about that encounter, and others like it, as intensely relevant to my column from a few weeks ago—on the failure of the Second Vatican Council to equip the church for the challenges of late modernity, the way its reforms aimed at resilience but led to crisis and diminishment instead.

What I tried to emphasize there, with some nods to the work of the French historian Guillaume Cuchet,[1] was that the problem with Vatican II probably wasn't any given change, any specific controversy that followed—whether over religious liberty or the use of

---

1. See chapter 17.

the vernacular in the liturgy or the moral status of artificial birth control. It was instead the sheer scale of the changes, the evisceration of a whole "culture of obligatory practice" (Cuchet's phrase), which severed various threads binding people to the faith, undermined confidence that the church really knew what it was doing and made people more dismissive of the obligations that officially remained.

The question of Sunday Mass-going is a good example. Technically, the church never said what my friendly interlocutor believed, never lifted the weekly obligation. But when an array of customs that reinforced that obligation were relaxed, from the requirement to fast before Mass to the emphasis on regular confession, the tacit message was the one he received—that the time of stringent rules was over, that henceforth the church would be defined by a more, well, American sort of flexibility.

The idea was not simply to make Catholicism easier, of course; the hope was that a truer Christianity would flourish once rote obedience diminished. But the policy and the results, not the hopes, are what we should be interested in three generations later. And in and of itself, a policy of easing burdens was hardly a crazy idea of how the church might adapt to modernity and keep Catholics in the pews. Spiritual issues aside, from an institutional perspective, you can see the logic of saying, *the world is making it harder to be a Catholic, so let's make it easier to practice the faith.*

Indeed, I will say that the relaxed style of the contemporary church offers useful concessions to my own situation as a busy professional juggling an assortment of secular obligations for myself and my family, and operating in numerous environments—familial, social and professional—where many people aren't Catholics.

But I'm also an unusual case: a teenage convert and a convert's son, an overly intellectualized believer, a bit of a weirdo in my mixture of laxness and literalism.

For most people, Catholic faith isn't an idea you've chosen that then has corollaries in practice (like *get to Mass on Sunday*). It's an inheritance that you get handed and have to decide what to do with. And the foundational problem with the keep-people-Catholic-by-making-it-easier-to-be-Catholic approach, it turns out, is that it removes too many of the signals indicating that this part of your inheritance is important—essential—rather than something you can keep without really investing in it, for yourself or, when the time comes, for your kids.

From this perspective, a key obstacle to getting modern Catholics to actually practice their inherited Catholicism isn't whether they disagree with church teachings or feel adequately welcomed (as much as those issues matter). It's that the church is in competition with a million other urgent-seeming things, and in its post-Vatican II form it has often failed to establish the importance of its own rituals and obligations.

For example, my guess would be that more American Catholics skip Mass because of the demands of youth sports, the felt need for a more relaxed "family time" or the competing pulls of work and entertainment than because of any theological or moral issue. And over time, this pattern compounds: The children of those families become couples who don't bother to marry in the church and parents who don't baptize their kids, and so decline continues because of cultural priorities rather than beliefs.

Right now, Catholic officialdom is engaged in a so-called synod on synodality, a series of listening sessions and bureaucratic confabs aimed at making the church more welcoming and inclusive—with a strong suspicion from conservatives that the endgame is further liberalizations of church doctrine.

I'm one of those suspicious conservatives, but I think the analysis of Vatican II I'm offering here points to a slightly different set of questions for the liberal Catholics who are having their hour under Pope Francis. Namely, which of their reforms would make the church seem more *important* to the semi-lapsed? How do you reach someone who doesn't feel unwelcome at Mass but also doesn't feel any kind of urgency about attending? If progressive Catholicism is in the business of lifting what it sees as nonessential obligations, hastening toward a possible future where one need not even be Catholic to receive communion in the Catholic Church, what form of obligation can it then instill?

The liberalizers don't believe that a return to tradition suffices for the present challenge. Very well; as a non-traditionalist in my own practice, I'm evidence for their point. But what is the novel means, the welcoming and affirming 21st-century mechanism, whereby my friend from the party, the ancestral Catholic, can be persuaded that it really, truly matters whether he shows up to Sunday Mass?

Any potential recovery of Catholic vitality under the Pope Francis model, any future where the revolution of Vatican II is somehow vindicated after all, hinges above all on the answer to that question.

Of course, all of the foregoing assumes my original premise, that Catholic decline since Vatican II is so substantial as to undermine various attempts (by John Paul II conservatives as well as liberals) to treat the council as a great success. But the premise itself is certainly contested. For instance, by Cardinal Jean-Claude Hollerich, a key Francis ally and possible successor, who recently told a Spanish newspaper, "if we did not have that point of reform that was the Second Vatican Council, the church today would be a small sect, unknown to most people."

I'll grant that Roman Catholicism isn't "unknown" in the current era. But in Hollerich's region of Europe (he is the archbishop of Luxembourg), it already *is* a "small sect" by the standards of the past: Some reports have put Mass attendance among self-identified Catholics in Germany at around 9 percent, and around 5 percent among Dutch and French Catholics, all part of a steep multigenerational decline. Any secular organization that conducted a sweeping renewal effort that yielded such results would know exactly what to think; any claim that *but for those reforms we'd be at 1 percent rather than 5 percent* would not be taken seriously.

For a more detailed, less facially implausible argument, I recommend the Twitter thread from David Gibson, the director of Fordham University's Center on Religion and Culture, replying to my column. His strongest argument is about the post–Vatican II vitality of Catholicism outside of the West. This vitality is primarily visible in sub-Saharan Africa, where Catholicism has grown dramatically as the continent's population has boomed, without the dramatic falling-off that you see elsewhere. Is this due to Vatican II enabling, as Gibson puts it, the "promotion of inculturation and vernacular liturgies," rather than a stuffy Eurocentric Latin? Or is it part of a wider exceptionalism in much of sub-Saharan Africa to conventional expectations about modernization and secularization, which would have obtained absent the council's reforms? I don't think we know, but I grant that the African story cries out for deeper study and complicates any critique of Vatican II.

But the exception is Africa, not, as Gibson suggests, some general "global South" that what he calls my "parochial" American perspective ignores. Yes, it's likely that demographic momentum carried Catholic growth forward in some parts of the world even as the steep decline began in the West, but the patterns in Latin America are now similar to American and European patterns, except with more losses to Pentecostalism and evangelicalism. (Just between 2010 and 2020, in the pope's native Argentina, the share of Catholic identifiers went from 76 percent to 49 percent of the population.) The post-1960s collapse is worst in Western Europe, but the failure of renewal is evident almost everywhere that Catholicism was well-established before the council.

Then Gibson's other points are less convincing: He accuses me of lacking "a sense of history" for not acknowledging that the challenges facing the church run deeper than the council. But my column explicitly stated that some version of Vatican II was necessary, that its unfortunate failure does not prove the church could have just continued as it was without facing some sort of crisis, some shock or decline.

He argues that American Catholicism has been "surprisingly resilient" and that "it is likely that the reforms that followed Vatican II enlivened the church in the U.S. considerably and continue to bear fruit." But American resilience arguably cuts against his argument, since progressive Catholics frequently argue that Catholicism in the United States remains too traditionalist, hidebound, even "integralist," that it hasn't gone far enough in the true implementation of Vatican II.

He invokes the chaos that followed past councils to say that by my lights quite a few would have to be "reckoned a failure," and yes, I think some of them were. Does anyone believe, for instance, that the Fifth Lateran Council of 1512–1517 needs to be held up as a great work of the Holy Spirit when it clearly failed to do anything useful to prevent the Protestant Reformation that began the year it ended?

Even the Council of Trent plainly failed in some of its objectives, since it did not reconcile Lutherans or re-Catholicize Northern Europe or prevent the Thirty Years' War. (Though if you believe the current condition of Western Catholic practice and culture will someday be favorably compared to the saints and artists and theologians of the Counter-Reformation era, I have a bridge between the Vatican and Jerusalem I'd like to sell you.)

Finally, Gibson concludes, "at some point a Catholic has to believe that a Council (or synod) is at some level a work of the Spirit and not simply a partisan campaign pitting one agenda against another. That is literally un-Catholic and leads only to cynicism, and bad takes." I agree with the "at some level" part; for instance, I think you can see the Holy Spirit at work in the Second Vatican Council's effect on Catholic-Jewish relations alone. But I emphatically don't agree with the implication that councils and synods can't be judged and found wanting in their most important practical effects. I doubt Gibson believes this either—unless he takes a very different perspective on, say, the medieval crusades and the councils that encouraged them than the median liberal Catholic.

Ultimately, the business of the Catholic Church is to save souls, to serve Jesus Christ and to manifest the presence of God through its holiness and beauty. And as I said in the column, and I'll say again: What really breeds cynicism is when the church behaves like the Soviet empire in its dotage and demands constant encomiums to the wisdom and success of a now decades-old renewal project, when everyone can plainly see it's presiding over crisis and decline.

13

Learning to Situate
the Post-War Council

TIMOTHY S. FLANDERS

OnePeterFive
October 18, 2022

SIXTY YEARS AGO THIS MONTH, PAPA RONCALLI WAS carried into the Second Vatican Council after an hours-long procession and then delivered the famous speech with which that council opened.

I believe that in time, historians will call this event the "post-war council." Why? Because the Council was dominated by the post-World War II context and, specifically, by narratives created by two victorious countries we will discuss below. The term, which I owe to Kennedy Hall, is helpful for a number of reasons. It allows us to achieve a sympathetic understanding of why there was so much optimism at the Council. For us, a few generations removed from the Second Sexual Revolution (1968–1973), mired in the holocaust of the unborn, the optimism of Vatican II sounds like so many hippies scratching painted nails down Fulton Sheen's chalkboard. However, if we understand better the post-war milieu, we can get a grip on those "signs of the times" that were dominant in the minds of the majority of Council Fathers and their supporters. The term "post-war council" helps us to understand the historical epoch that *came and went* before 1968 vomited forth the errors of Russia all over Western Europe and the Americas; it reaches the heart of the situation that many good churchmen were facing—and that nefarious actors exploited.

One could reasonably assert that the moment of 1962–1965 was the *opportune moment* to win over modern man with the medicine of mercy. In fact, it was Pius XII who began this dialogue and who understood this *kairos* moment (with important precedents to be found in Pius VII, Leo XIII, and Pius XI).[1] According to this view, the "modern man" of whom the Council speaks should be understood specifically as *post-war* man. I will use both phrases synonymously.

Yet one can also reasonably assert, as I will explain, that that moment has come and gone. Post-war man no longer exists. If the conditions present in 1962 could reasonably have justified some sort of optimism (albeit tenuous and fragile), the fact that those conditions are no longer present make the opposite conclusion—that the time for conciliar optimism is definitely over and done with—*necessarily also reasonable*. We can see this more clearly if we delve into post-war narratives and milieus in France and the American Empire.

The post-war narrative

First, we need to disentangle a difficult topic: *the post-war narrative*, namely, the propaganda history told by the victorious Allies after World War II, which was critically influential at Vatican II. Unfortunately, most of us are still being taught the post-war narrative, even in Catholic homeschool programs. So some of what follows might come as a shock to certain readers.

The most basic narrative is that World War II was an epic battle of good (Allies) vs. evil (Axis). History is written by the victors, and this version is particularly lazy. Because of the magnitude of evil on the Axis side, it was easy for the Allied powers to believe such an oversimplification of the truth, as many in the Anglophone universe still do. In reality, World War II is better characterized as "a mass murderer and his Allies against a mass murderer and his Axis."[2] Or more potently (and in line with the message of Fatima), Christopher Dawson called the war *The Judgment of the Nations*, in a book of the same name he wrote during it.

---

1. Bishop Chiaramonti's positive evaluation of the French revolutionaries taking over Italy and (as Pius VII) his subsequent ambiguous concordat with Napoleon; Leo XIII's whole *ralliement* project and positive evaluation of the providence of the United States; and Pius XI's suppression of *Action Française*.

2. See T. S. Flanders, *City of God vs. City of Man* (n.p.: Our Lady of Victory Press, 2021), 396–407.

A single world war with a decades-long ceasefire

Some historians consider the period from 1914 to 1945 as a single war, interrupted by a lengthy ceasefire. Versailles—Martinmas, 1918 "Armistice Day," "Remembrance Day," "Veterans Day"—was *not* a peace treaty. It was a ceasefire. St. Augustine defines peace as *the tranquility of order.* Therefore a peace treaty is and should be a *just peace* that restores justice, as much as possible, to all sides so that the *cause* of war may be eliminated. This was the aim of Bl. Emperor Karl, the model layman of the twentieth century. He sought a truly just peace that would give to his enemies, the Allies of the Great War (1914–1918), their own just claims on territory and give to his people their own just demands, and for this cause he was willing to give up disputed areas and negotiate in good faith.

The Versailles treaty punished Germany for no other reason than to take revenge for the Franco-Prussian War, for their hubris in challenging the British Navy, and for their atrocities. Benedict XV rightly called the Great War a "carnage solely for economic reasons."[3] The interwar period helped to create the First Sexual Revolution (1918–1929) as well as Soviet-fueled Communist revolutionary fervor everywhere, provoking a reaction from World War I veterans. One of these veterans, as we know, embraced the eugenics of the American Empire, mixed with a demonic neo-Paganism, and created the scourge of National Socialism. Meanwhile, the American Empire sided with the Soviet Empire against Christendom in the brutal slaughter of priests and nuns, which created countless martyrs in the conflict known as the Spanish Civil War (1936–1939). This merely manifested the way in which Russia's errors fit with American (exported) Liberalism hand-in-glove, militarily, economically, and morally.

During this period, Our Lady of Fatima showed to the world the path of a *just* peace: penance, penance, penance! But there was no consecration of Russia by Pius XI, and not enough penance. So God removed his protecting hand from Europe and the world. Spurred on by the fallen angels, the two mass murderers Stalin and Hitler at

---

3. Pope Benedict XV, Peace Plan.

first signed an agreement to conquer and divide Eastern Europe between themselves in order to build up their respective empires. When Hitler betrayed Stalin, France and Britain found themselves as Stalin's allies, with the American Empire soon to follow.

Post-war man is born to a new hope

When France and the American Empire again emerged victorious over Germany, a few things were different about the post-war situation, contributing to an immense optimism.

First, the magnitude of the evil in the Nazi regime made the victorious Allies into true liberators of France and West Germany. Hitler was indeed an insane neo-pagan, and thus his defeat was an unequivocal good. That was the element of truth sustaining the victors' narrative.

Second, the Holy See had definitely turned in favor of the Allies' system of Liberalism, in a way it had not done during the Great War. As Pius XII said at Christmas in 1944, in an address that would later be cited by Vatican II:

> Out from the mournful groans of sorrow, from the very depths of the heart-rending anguish of oppressed individuals and countries, there arises an aura of hope. To an ever-increasing number of noble souls there comes the thought, the will, ever clearer and stronger, to make of this world, this universal upheaval, a starting point for a new era of far-reaching renovation, the complete reorganization of the world. . . .
>
> Moreover—and this is perhaps the most important point— beneath the sinister lightning of the war that encompasses them, in the blazing heat of the furnace that imprisons them, the peoples have, as it were, awakened from a long torpor. They have assumed, in relation to the state and those who govern, a new attitude—one that questions, criticizes, distrusts.
>
> Taught by bitter experience, they are more aggressive in opposing the concentration of dictatorial power that cannot be censured or touched, and call for a system of government more in keeping with the dignity and liberty of the citizens. These multitudes, uneasy, stirred by the war to their innermost depths, are today firmly convinced—at first, perhaps, in a vague and confused way, but already unyieldingly—that had there been the possibility of

censuring and correcting the actions of public authority, the world would not have been dragged into the vortex of a disastrous war, and that to avoid for the future the repetition of such a catastrophe, we must vest efficient guarantees in the people itself.

In such a psychological atmosphere, is it to be wondered at if the tendency towards democracy is capturing the peoples and winning a large measure of consent and support from those who hope to play a more effective part in the destinies of individuals and of society?

This turn was similar to Pius XI's condemnation of *Action Française* in the sense that it gave to the churchmen who were promoters of Leo XIII's *ralliement* with post-1773 Liberalism an official promotion by the highest authority in the Church.

A third critically important piece of this optimism lies in the fact that, to its credit, the American Empire quickly broke its wartime alliance with the Soviets and openly declared an ideological crusade on Communism. This was a welcome shift from the previous ambiguous stance toward the errors of Russia that the United States had taken after the Great War, when its global promotion of Liberalism had facilitated (and funded) the Bolshevik horror.

Finally, on the popular level, the 1950s saw American popular culture, which had previously been exporting jazzified fornication in the 1920s, produce Ven. Fulton Sheen on primetime television. He manifested a virulently Catholic *and* patriotic spirit in the quasi-religious crusade against the errors of Russia. Meanwhile, Hollywood exported Catholic films for the big screen like *The Miracle of Our Lady of Fatima* (Warner Bros., 1952); the stereotypical American pop culture prized the heterosexual nuclear family and strong father. The Catholic-led "Legion of Decency" had eradicated the 1920s pornography from Hollywood and the global dominance of American film produced stories of heroic priests and nuns. If we know the historical context, it shouldn't surprise us that Jacques Maritain could write in 1956:

> It will be necessary for the European spirit and the American spirit to meet and cooperate in common good will . . . what the world expects from America is that she keep alive, in human history, a

fraternal recognition of the dignity of man—in other words, the terrestrial hope of men in the Gospel.[4]

Perhaps more than any other, it was Jacques Maritain—the French Thomist who emigrated to the United States, writing *Integral Humanism* in 1936—who influenced the optimism of Vatican II, through two successive Francophile popes, John XXIII and Paul VI.[5] At that moment, Catholics—especially Catholics in the post-war countries liberated by the United States—knew the evil of National Socialism and Bolshevik Socialism alike. Both regimes crushed the individual person under the titanic machinery of state control. The American message of "all men are created equal" with its localized freedom, adorned with a Catholic popular face and breathing fierceness against the Soviets, was enough to convince many that the Church should expand on what Pius XII said and, at last, formally engage in a new dialogue with Modernity. To top it all off, in 1960 the American Empire elected an Irish-American Catholic president, John F. Kennedy.

This is why it is reasonable to assert that the period of the early sixties was truly an opportune moment to win over post-war man to the Gospel—for it seemed as if the Americans were already working in this direction, and an Ecumenical Council could only advance and deepen the campaign of rechristianization! Here we find the context to understand sympathetically John XXIII's "medicine of mercy" speech. No wonder he thought that "man of himself is inclined to condemn his own errors." By electing Kennedy, millions of Americans had put aside their generations-long anti-Irish and anti-Catholic prejudice.[6] Further, the post-war countries were

---

4. Jacques Maritain, *Reflections on America* (New York: Scribner, 1958).

5. We can also see how Maritain, having come from the bitterly divided, post-Dreyfus France, could be so impressed by a 1930s United States with its Catholic dominance leading a "true Ecumenism" in the Legion of Decency. On Paul VI's penchant for modern French thought, see Yves Chiron's detailed biography *Paul VI: The Divided Pope*, trans. James Walther (Brooklyn, NY: Angelico Press, 2022).

6. Even though Kennedy had to all but explicitly renounce his Faith to become president. See my article "The Conflicted Legacy of American Catholicism," *One PeterFive*, April 21, 2020, https://onepeterfive.com/conflicted-american-catholicism.

firmly committed to preventing another war, and thus the pope's speech talked about how men everywhere condemned "fratricidal wars" and "the might of arms." Indeed, the peaceful resolution of the Cuban Missile Crisis, which took place during the First Session less than a week after this speech, seemed to confirm before their very eyes that post-war man had truly matured after the bloodbath of World War II. Pope John's inspiration was the Council of Trent, and his 1960 Roman Synod, as a model for Vatican II, sought to republish the Catechism of Trent and win over post-war man to take the final step to be fully Catholic.[7]

We will have a still better insight into Vatican II's optimism if we consider two post-war countries of outsized influence at the Council.

Post-war France: the triumph of the generation of 1930

Dr. Jon Kirwan's *An Avant-garde Theological Generation: The Nouvelle Théologie and the French Crisis of Modernity* describes in great detail how the interwar period helped to form and shape the "generation of 1930" (born between 1895 and 1905): men like Henri de Lubac, Yves Congar, and Marie-Dominique Chenu, all of them influential figures later on at Vatican II. Their optimism reflected the thought of Maurice Blondel, Teilhard de Chardin, and Jacques Maritain, among others.

Before World War II, ideas of an optimistic dialogue with Modernity were controversial in the Church. During the Nazi occupation, however, these figures and their students were on the forefront of the French Resistance, fighting alongside French Communists and other Liberals under Charles de Gaulle. Meanwhile, an older generation led by Marshall Pétain favored a tenuous peace with Hitler under ideals diametrically opposed to Modernity. After Hitler was defeated, the Generation of 1930 seemed to be totally vindicated. Kirwan elaborates:

---

7. For a traditionalist perspective on Papa Roncalli, see Henry Sire's *Phoenix from the Ashes* and Romano Amerio's *Iota Unum*. On Trent as an inspiration for Roncalli, see Jared Wicks, SJ, *Investigating Vatican II: Its Theologians, Ecumenical Turn, and Biblical Commitment* (Washington, DC: CUA Press, 2018).

[By] May 1945, the intellectual lines that would shape post-war France were already laid by the three parties that emerged from the war as victors: Communists, existentialists, and Left Catholics [*nouvelle théologie*].... A "cultural power vacuum" had been created by the fall of the Republic. The political and Catholic Right had been discredited, by a real or perceived support for the Vichy regime, as well as the older generation, for its association with the failed Third Republic. The left-wing intellectuals, philosophers, writers, and theologians of the generation of 1930, whose intellectual projects had matured during the previous decade, found themselves heroically legitimized by their opposition to Vichy and participation in the Resistance, and they stepped into a virtually uncontested void in full intellectual ferment.[8]

In the words of one young priest on the day after the Liberation, describing the shift from Pétain's regime to de Gaulle's new post-war France:

It is not a change in government which has just happened: it is really something quite different! It is the Liberation of France, it is a revolution! It is not only the Germans who are going, it is those who desired their victory. And for the common people, it is hope which is arriving with General de Gaulle, hope for more justice and dignity. For France, it is a new beginning.[9]

The leader of the old regime, who symbolized the older generation, was sentenced to death for treason, but his sentence was commuted to life in prison. After 1945, opinion in the Church swung strongly in favor of the generation of 1930 and their positive dialogue with Modernity. This received a huge boost when the two Francophile popes were elected, one after the other. Given the historical context, one can understand why Catholics of good will were caught up in the euphoria. Nevertheless, looked at more soberly, the ferment consisted of a mixture of naïveté, a structure of neoscholasticism, the reality of true liberation and hope for new freedom,

---

8. Jon Kirwan, *An Avant-garde Theological Generation: The Nouvelle Theologie and the French Crisis of Modernity* (New York: Oxford University Press, 2018), 233–34.

9. Jean Vinatier, *Le Cardinal Suhard* (Paris: Le Centurion, 1983), 204–5, cited in Kirwan, *Avant-garde Theological Generation*, 234.

Masonic-Marxist infiltration, and a resurgence of old-style modernism. It was a collection of half-truths informed by the post-war narrative. There was enough truth in this narrative to make men of good will think it might turn out well—but enough ambiguity and error to make the gamble dangerous.

These French theologians, de Lubac chief among them, provided inspiration for people like Joseph Ratzinger and Karol Wojtyla, who had fought against the Nazis or Soviets in their own way. The Maritain/Teilhard theories of optimistic evolution only provided momentum for the momentary *Weltanschauung* of "all things liberation."[10]

Post-war America: global psychological warfare

Meanwhile, the American Empire was launching the most sophisticated global psychological warfare project in the history of mankind. No scholar has laid this out better than David Wemhoff in his book *John Courtney Murray, Time/Life, and The American Proposition: How the CIA's Doctrinal Warfare Program Changed the Catholic Church* (South Bend: Wagon Wheel Press, 2022). Just as the Soviet Empire was targeting the Catholic Church with infiltration, so too, the American Empire sought to convince the Catholic Church to endorse America-style Liberalism by the use of what the CIA termed "doctrinal warfare."[11] No wonder Pope Benedict XVI could later say of this time and its influence on Vatican II:

---

10. In fact, Kirwan notes how the infamous godfather of Liberation Theology, Gustavo Gutiérrez, was himself inspired and influenced by this "French liberation moment." Peter Seewald in his *Benedict XVI: A Life*, vol. 1, describes how the French resistance inspired Joseph Ratzinger to embrace the priesthood. What Plinio Corrêa de Oliveira said of France was certainly true of the post-war milieu: "Every people has its own food, wine, dress, perfumes, etc. but when the French touch them, they take on a higher form and become a model for others. . . . The others [nations] naturally tend to follow its example" ("Vocations of the European Peoples," www.traditioninaction.org/OrganicSociety/A_006_Vocations_PCO.htm).

11. "PSB Planning Objectives" Top Secret [Declassified 1998], April 7, 1952, "Doctrinal Warfare" Memoranda, "Psychological Strategy Planning for Western Europe" and "Latin America," Jan.-Feb. 1953, *Dwight D. Eisenhower Library*, in David Wemhoff, *John Courtney Murray* (n.p.: Fidelity Press, 2015), 278–319.

People came to realize that the American Revolution was offering a model of a modern State that differed from the theoretical model with radical tendencies that had emerged during the second phase of the French Revolution.... Catholic statesmen demonstrated that a modern secular State could exist that was not neutral regarding values but alive, drawing from the great ethical sources opened by Christianity.[12]

The difficulty here is that we are dealing with yet another half-truth informed by the post-war narrative. The United States was, in a way, actually promoting Catholicism (at least on the popular level) and waging ideological war against Communism; and *some* aspects of the fundamental Christian concept of the *imago Dei*, held against both the Soviets and the vanquished Nazis, could be found in *some* aspects of American ideals. But these goods were fatally mixed in with an anti-Christian, indeed anti-human, Liberalism.

As Vatican II drew closer, international media also began to televise the struggle of black Americans against unjust laws in the Jim Crow South, which formed a parallel youth movement to French resistance against the Nazis (as well as the youthful Worker Priest evangelization effort). As mentioned before, a Catholic president was elected in 1960 who famously threw his support behind a jailed Martin Luther King Jr. during the election. Kennedy's "martyr's death" in 1963 was followed by national mourning, and by 1964— during the Third Session of Vatican II—King was awarded the Nobel Peace prize. Vatican II seemed to be looking directly at the most positive elements in post-war France and the United States when it said in the next year in 1965, echoing Pius XII:

Modern man is on the road to a more thorough development of his own personality, and to a growing discovery and vindication of his own rights.... [Yet] by no human law can the personal dignity and liberty of man be so aptly safeguarded as by the Gospel of Christ which has been entrusted to the Church. For this Gospel announces and proclaims the freedom of the sons of God, and repudiates all the bondage which ultimately results from sin....

The Church, therefore, by virtue of the Gospel committed to

12. Benedict XVI, Christmas Address to the Roman Curia, December 22, 2005.

her, proclaims the rights of man; she acknowledges and greatly esteems the dynamic movements of today by which these rights are everywhere fostered. Yet these movements must be penetrated by the spirit of the Gospel and protected against any kind of false autonomy. For we are tempted to think that our personal rights are fully ensured only when we are exempt from every requirement of divine law. But this way lies not the maintenance of the dignity of the human person, but its annihilation.[13]

This passage seems to sum up the post-war optimism of Vatican II and the olive branch of the medicine of mercy offered by the Church, but at the same time issues a warning of what might happen if this olive branch of dialogue were to be refused by modern man; it would be nothing less than the "annihilation" of the human person. A similar warning is contained in another passage of Vatican II, perhaps due to the salutary traditional influence of the *Coetus Internationalis Patrum*:[14]

In our own time, moreover, those who have trusted excessively in the progress of the natural sciences and the technical arts have fallen into an idolatry of temporal things and have become their slaves rather than their masters.[15]

Our traditionalist godfathers in the *Coetus* were among the few who could see through the shallow optimism and half-truths of the post-war narrative. A salutary passage like this one was promulgated but quickly fell on deaf ears, swallowed up in an optimism running headlong into the arms of the world, the flesh, and the devil. The post-war narrative provided enough truth ("cover," one might say) to convince many, but also enough programmatic ambiguity to make the Vatican II project vulnerable to hijacking by the enemies of Christ and His Church.

---

13. Second Vatican Council, Pastoral Constitution on the Church in the Modern World *Gaudium et Spes*, 41.

14. The key "integralist" phrase contained in the first paragraph of *Dignitatis Humanae* is indeed the work of the *Coetus*, according to the biography of Archbishop Lefebvre.

15. Second Vatican Council, Decree on the Apostolate of the Laity *Apostolicam Actuositatem*, 7.

Post-war man rejecting Vatican II

Already in 1964, while post-war churchmen were focused on the Council's grand hopes, Hollywood had produced the first pornographic film since the 1920s. In 1967, then-Father Theodore McCarrick was signing the "Land O' Lakes Statement"—in some ways, the death-knell of the enormously successful Catholic educational system in the USA—and, after the delayed and unsupported release of *Humanae Vitae* in 1968, priests and bishops joined the Second Sexual Revolution in open revolt against perennial Catholic doctrine.

The reality is that modern man, post-war man, utterly rejected the Church's olive branch of mercy, and then imposed upon the world the unspeakable holocaust of the unborn, by far the greatest concentration of evil brutality against human dignity that the world has ever known. Whatever was good in the post-war milieu about liberating man from the evils of Communism and National Socialism soured and curdled into the "annihilation" of the human person, even in the sanctuary of the womb. Vatican II offered mercy to modernity, and modernity rejected it.

Pope Francis is concerned with Catholic traditionalists who, he claims, reject Vatican II. But before traditionalism ever existed as a broad movement, *modern man had rejected Vatican II*. And that's the point. That's what the traditionalists have been saying, in many and varied ways, about the *deficiency* of Vatican II. Even if we were to assert, for the sake of argument, that Vatican II's doctrinal orthodoxy is absolutely crystal-clear, we would also have to assert that the pastoral program to win over modern man with mercy has been a failure because modern man, in the satanic exultation of Liberalism, rejected it.

After the Second Sexual Revolution began, modern post-war man became *postmodern self-warring man*. He has surrendered himself to neopaganism to offer the blood of his sons and his daughters to devils (see Ps. 105:37). He is warring against himself, his own nature, his sexual identity, his governance by the natural law, his place in creation, his need for redemption. The world—and the pastoral situation—has radically and completely changed from the heady days of John F. Kennedy. Dr. R. Jared Staudt wrote this cogent assessment:

In the end, the Church will have to discern whether or not the vision of Vatican II is adequate for leading the Church to the renewal in mission so desperately needed as she continues to decline throughout most of the world. Beyond rejecting the legitimacy of Vatican II and its teaching, it is a different matter to question the effectiveness of its pastoral strategy and its continued relevance for pointing the Church toward the future.[16]

When we look at the post-war milieu, we can see why many churchmen felt this immense optimism. We could even assert, although it would be difficult to prove historically, that this was indeed the opportune moment for the medicine of mercy, a "Constantinian moment" when Western, secular democracy might have embraced the Faith. But we can also look around us and see without difficulty that post-war man has been transformed into post-modern, post-human man who denies his own nature and his sex and reality itself.[17] Catholics of good will must be honest enough to admit that it was the godfathers of traditionalism—the *Coetus Internationalis Patrum*, led, in fact, by Archbishop Marcel Lefebvre—who warned about this situation at Vatican II itself, and who were generally ignored or ridiculed. We might reasonably concede that the optimism project could have worked, if post-war man had accepted it; but we must also admit that it did not succeed, because he did not "know the time of his visitation," to use the words of Our Lord about faithless Jerusalem. The "prophets of doom" excoriated by John XXIII proved to be correct in their caution. And no Catholic is being "unfaithful to the Church" for following the Second Vatican Council's own exhortation to "read the signs of the times," of *these* times, *our* times.

For our times are no longer the post-war epoch. 2022 is not 1962. We live in the age of the holocaust of the unborn. The globalist conspiracy of the fallen angels. The slavery of social media and the

---

16. R. Jared Staudt, "What does it mean to reject Vatican II?," *Catholic World Report*, July 7, 2022, www.catholicworldreport.com/2022/07/07/what-does-it-mean-to-reject-vatican-ii.

17. See Rafael Xavier Gonzalez, "Posthumanism and Theological Anthropology," *OnePeterFive*, July 7, 2022, https://onepeterfive.com/posthumanism-and-theological-anthropology.

human trafficking of international pornography. The Ukraine crisis and the threat of global nuclear war. Let us not be so naïve as to offer the medicine of mercy to the Antichrist.

14

A Window into the
Post-Vatican II Liturgical Reforms

MATTHEW HAZELL

New Liturgical Movement
October 22, 2022

THE SIXTIETH ANNIVERSARY OF THE OPENING OF THE
Second Vatican Council (October 11, 1962) has recently passed,
accompanied with the usual panegyrics and plaudits, this time
around with the addition of so-called "synodality." Indeed, we
should, so the Pope says, "return to the Council's pure sources of
love . . . rediscover the Council's passion and renew our own passion for the Council."

I thought, then, that it would be perfectly in keeping with the
Pope's words to look at what the Council Fathers *actually* had to say
about the Constitution on the Sacred Liturgy, beginning with the
man who would be elected as Supreme Pontiff in 1963: the then-
Archbishop of Milan, Giovanni Battista Cardinal Montini.

Sixty years ago today [October 22], Cardinal Montini gave a spoken intervention on the floor of the Council, in which, with the
benefit of hindsight, we are given a window into the postconciliar
liturgical reforms and how *Sacrosanctum Concilium* would be
applied by the future Pope and the *Consilium ad exsequendam*. In
this speech, we can see a *via media* expressed by Montini: he wishes
Latin to be preserved in the "priestly parts" of the liturgy, but vernacular for the "didactic parts"; damaging "innovations" are to be
avoided, but "prudent" and "wise" changes to the liturgy are necessary for the "men of our age." Of course, this 'middle way' did not
come to pass: Montini's own conviction that "the Liturgy was instituted for men, not men for the Liturgy," as well as his principle that
"the greatest pastoral efficacy . . . be given to the Sacred Liturgy,"

would seem, in the end, to have overruled almost every other consideration, and opened the way for exactly the sorts of "fickle, damaging innovations" he declared himself to be against in 1962.

Still, with regard to Montini's *via media*, others would express similar intentions about, for example, the question of Latin and the vernacular, and notably it was what the Council Fathers were *specifically told* that *Sacrosanctum Concilium* nn. 36 and 54 meant:

> Article [36], as it is in the schema, is the best way to follow the *via media* between the two extremes. . . .[1]

> Regarding article n. 41, now n. 54. . . . Others judge that the entire Mass is to be said in the vernacular. But exiling Latin from the Mass contradicts the principle already established in article 36. . . . Rather, we ought to walk by the *via media*. . . .[2]

That these intentions were later ignored and abandoned by the Consilium and Paul VI should prove, contrary to various recent assertions (notably *Desiderio Desideravi*, n. 31), that to question the post-Vatican II reforms is in no way to "reject" the Council, whatever *that* means![3] And readers of NLM should remember, particularly over the next year when, no doubt, much will be written about "the Council" and the "spirit of Vatican II," that the *Acta Synodalia* demonstrate the accuracy of Cardinal Ratzinger's words in 1976:

> The problem of the new Missal lies in its abandonment of a historical process that was always continual, before and after St. Pius V, and in the creation of a completely new book, although it was compiled of old material, the publication of which was accompanied by a prohibition of all that came before it, which, besides, is unheard of in the history of both law and liturgy. And I can say with certainty, based on my knowledge of the conciliar debates and my repeated reading of the speeches made by the Council

---

1. *Relatio*, General Congregation XXXIV, December 5, 1962: *Acta Synodalia* I.4:285.

2. *Relatio*, General Congregation XLIII, October 8, 1963: *Acta Synodalia* II.2:290.

3. See Alcuin Reid, "Does *Traditionis Custodes* Pass Liturgical History 101?," in Peter A. Kwasniewski, ed., *From Benedict's Peace to Francis's War: Catholics Respond to the Motu Proprio* Traditionis Custodes *on the Latin Mass* (Brooklyn, NY: Angelico Press, 2021), 252–59.

Fathers, that this does not correspond to the intentions of the Second Vatican Council.[4]

* * *

Giovanni Battista Cardinal Montini, Archbishop of Milan
Spoken Intervention on *Sacrosanctum Concilium*
Given at the Second Vatican Council,
General Congregation IV, 22nd October 1962[5]

May I also, as metropolitan of the region of Lombardy and moderator of the Ambrosian rite, openly pledge that I approve the proposed schema as to its substance, and ask this very large group of Fathers to favor the principle on which, it seems to me, the whole schema is based: the principle that the greatest pastoral efficacy may be given to the Sacred Liturgy.

In fact, the schema seems to highly recommend this, because of what is affirmed in paragraph n. 5, namely: "Although the sacred Liturgy does not include the whole sphere of the activity of the Church, it is nevertheless at her center, which is the Divine Eucharistic Sacrifice, the summit to which all things must be directed, and at the same time from which all things proceed."[6]

Therefore, in this outline of the sacred Liturgy, viewed as a whole, there is a true balance, I think, between two judgments which equally serve the pastoral purpose of the Council, namely:

1. The schema is not of the kind to yield to those who want to introduce innovations with fickleness of mind and at their own discretion, or, worse still, cause damage to those highly esteemed things, divine and human, that are contained in the sacred Liturgy and which have been transmitted to the Christian people over the course of many centuries, preserving the authentic unity of this tra-

---

4. Joseph Ratzinger, letter to Wolfgang Waldstein, original German text in "Zum motu proprio *Summorum Pontificum*," *Una Voce Korrespondenz* 38/3 (2008), 201–14; translation by Peter Kwasniewski.

5. Latin text: *Acta Synodalia* I.1:311–13, translated by Matthew P. Hazell, with emphases and added notes.

6. This paragraph would later be developed and then split over nn. 9–10 of *Sacrosanctum Concilium* (*SC*).

dition as regards its substance. Those who follow the Ambrosian rite wish to present themselves, in a particular way, as faithful in regard to this.

2. Further, the schema does not favor the opinion of those who assert that the rite must be completely unchangeable, or who adhere too much to the ceremonies handed down by history, preferring the form in which the worship is expressed over the essentials signified by this very form.

And so the proposed schema appears to effect its purpose, so that it is constantly attached to two things: the essence of the Liturgy itself, which must be completely defended and preserved, and its traditional or historical form, that is, the way in which the celebration of the divine mysteries is, as it were, clothed; this form can indeed be changed, but prudently and wisely, and for more suitable reasons revived. The schema thus in no way diminishes the divine patrimony of Catholic worship, received from our forefathers, but it permits and recommends that the postconciliar commissions to be established—in which even bishops who are pastors of souls must be present—render this same patrimony more clearly, so that it is more comprehensible and useful to men of our age, to whom, as shepherds, we are bound by duty out of conscience.

Indeed, on account of our burden, for which we must protect the tradition of ecclesiastical forms, we may not detract from the even greater obligation that we owe to both God and Christ, as well as to the Christian people and men of our times. For we know that this society of ours, in so much crisis when it comes to religion, can still come today to Christ, to the Church, and to salvation, especially with the help of the liturgical word.

The following is to be examined: especially when it comes to the language to be used in worship, the use of the ancient language handed down by our ancestors, namely the Latin language, should for the Latin Church be firm and stable in those parts of the rite which are sacramental and properly and truly priestly. This must be done so that the unity of the Mystical Body at prayer, as well as the accuracy of the sacred formulas, is religiously observed. However, as far as the people are concerned, any difficulty in understanding can be removed in the didactic parts of the sacred Liturgy, and the faithful also given the opportunity to express in comprehensible words their prayers, in which they call upon God.

We must not forget Saint Paul's eloquent teachings in 1 Corinthians 14, that is to say, he affirms that he who prays in the Church must understand with his mind what he utters with his mouth, and must answer "Amen" knowing what he is saying. The Liturgy was instituted for men, not men for the Liturgy. It is the prayer of the Christian community; if we desire that this community not abandon our temples, but that they may willingly approach them, and there have the interior life of the soul formed and express their faith worthily, the hindrance of a language that cannot be understood, or is appropriate for only a very few, must be removed, prudently, but without delay or hesitation. Whatever does not attract our people to participate in divine worship but alienates them from it is to be examined, as is excellently stated in n. 24 of the constitution.[7]

The sentence of St Augustine himself is not in vain, which warns: "better that linguistic experts should find fault with us than that people should not understand" (*Enarrationes in Psalmos*, 138, 20).

Likewise, the principle of reducing ceremonies to a simpler form seems commendable to me, not in order to diminish the beauty and rich meaning of worship, but to ensure that the brevity of the ceremonies may be properly considered and that repetitions and all complications be avoided; the liturgical reform here announced is supported by this principle, very appropriate and in keeping with the character of the men of our age, even pious and faithful ones.

Now I would like to add some particular observations in writing, which are proposed to the relevant commission, especially concerning the liturgies of the religious orders; for I wish that, on p. 169, after n. 32,[8] mention should be made or a new paragraph introduced about these liturgies, properly revised if necessary, of exempt religious,[9] due to their historical importance and spiritual dignity. *Dixi.*

---

7. Equivalent to *SC*, n. 36.

8. Equivalent to *SC*, n. 41. The page reference is to the printed copy of the draft liturgy schema given to the Fathers.

9. See 1917 *Code of Canon Law*, can. 488, §2, and *passim*; also, 1983 *Code of Canon Law*, can. 591.

15

Vatican II: *Requiescat in Pace**

PETER A. KWASNIEWSKI

I

OBSERVERS OF THE VATICAN SCENE HAVE KNOWN FOR
several years now that we cannot expect Pope Francis, who is a
major cause of the problems under which the Church is suffering,
to be a major part of their solution. As more astute writers have
pointed out, however, this pontificate has been, in spite of its evils, a
tremendous gift of Divine Providence. For Francis has brought to a
clarity past any reasonable doubt—one might even say has intensi-
fied to a fever pitch—the utter bankruptcy of "Vatican II Catholicism," with its lightweight liturgy, its unserious opposition to the
world, the flesh, and the devil, and its continual compromise with
the reigning forces of liberalism.

I was once one of those Talmudic scholars who attempted to
square every circle in the sixteen documents of the Council. I
praised their textual orthodoxy and lamented their neglect or distortion at the hands of hijackers. I knew that the loyal Catholic
mentality always began its sentences "if only...": "If only the new
liturgy were properly celebrated..."; "If only the new *Catechism*

---

* This chapter combines extensively rewritten material from four previously
published articles: "RIP, Vatican II Catholicism (1962–2018)," *OnePeterFive*, October 9, 2018, https://onepeterfive.com/rip-vatican-ii-catholicism; "The Second Vatican Council Is Now Far Spent," *OnePeterFive*, December 11, 2019, https://
onepeterfive.com/council-far-spent; "Why Viganò's Critique of the Council Must
Be Taken Seriously," *OnePeterFive*, June 29, 2020, https://onepeterfive.com/vigano-
critique-council/; and "Why Vatican II Cannot Simply Be Forgotten, but Must Be
Remembered with Shame and Repentance," *LifeSiteNews*, August 3, 2020, www.li
fesitenews.com/blogs/why-vatican-ii-cannot-simply-be-forgotten-but-must-be-re
membered-with-shame-and-repentance.

were widely taught…"; "If only people everywhere could follow the lead of the great Polish pope" (and later, "the great German pope").

That's where I used to live. I have since moved on to a bigger and more beautiful dwelling called Catholic tradition. I was tired of living in the newly constructed, supposedly more energy-efficient and environmentally sound but in reality flimsy, drafty, fluorescent, insect-infested, falling-apart brutalist building produced by the only Ecumenical Council that made no solemn definitions and issued no solemn condemnations. I came to see, thanks to detailed studies by such authors as Ralph Wiltgen (*The Rhine Flows into the Tiber*), Michael Davies (*Pope John's Council*), Romano Amerio (*Iota Unum*), Christopher Ferrara (*The Great Façade*), Roberto de Mattei (*The Second Vatican Council: An Unwritten Story*), and Henry Sire (*Phoenix from the Ashes*),[1] that the hijackers were not the ones *after* the Council, but the ones *inside* the Council who cleverly steered it toward the progressivism and modernism they espoused, deliberately planting "time bombs" throughout the documents—ambiguous phrases that could be turned this way or that, and which *were* turned this way and that in the never-ending turf war between liberals and "conservatives" of every stripe, at every level.

I came to see that the problem *was* the new liturgy—not just the obviously bad manner in which it was being "celebrated" throughout the world, but the thing in and of itself, in the texts and rubrics of its official books.[2] The new *Catechism*, too, in its diffuse verbosity and its glossing over difficult points like the headship of the husband in marriage, was not the magic solution; indeed, on the matter of the death penalty it was demoted to the status of reflecting pool for the reigning Narcissus. Above all, I came to see that "just following the pope" wheresoever he may go, on land or over the sea or in the sky via airplane interviews, is not only *not* the solution, but an outsized part of the problem.[3] And what is that problem? The

---

1. Naturally, to these authors could be added a long string of publications by Archbishop Marcel Lefebvre.

2. See Peter Kwasniewski, *The Once and Future Roman Rite: Returning to the Traditional Latin Liturgy after Seventy Years of Exile* (Gastonia, NC: TAN Books, 2022).

3. See Peter Kwasniewski, *The Road from Hyperpapalism to Catholicism: Rethink-*

eclipse, in our times, of any coherent idea of what Catholicism is, has been, and will always be—the *willed* eclipse, since "men loved darkness rather than the light, for their works were evil" (Jn. 3:19).

The liturgy we were given by Paul VI, courtesy of Archbishop Bugnini and his all-star Consilium, is indeed a lightweight liturgy that cannot sustain the weight of God's glory or meet the weighty needs of the human soul. Many know nothing else, and their plight reminds one of the plight of those people in Soviet Russia waiting in long lines for their crust of bread. This is not what the liturgy of the Church offered to her people in ages past: it offered a royal banquet, a king's delight, a glimpse of heaven, fellowship with the saints and angels. I'm not saying preconciliar liturgy was always perfect, for we know it wasn't; but the rites of the Church possessed in themselves the *density and beauty* that made a rich liturgical life always possible and frequently attainable. Catholics who revert to the traditional liturgy often exclaim with amazement: "They took *that* away from us?!" Yes, they did. This incomparable school of prayer, this inflexible staff to support our weakness, this comforting beauty to lure our earthbound souls into heaven—this was taken away, and those who did it knew *exactly* what they were doing, and why.

Earlier I spoke of "unserious opposition to the world, the flesh, and the devil." This is the identifying mark of postconciliar Catholicism. *Oppose* the world? *Convert* the world? No, we have to *dialogue* with it, understand it, sympathize with it, come to terms with it, make common cause with it, recycle its garbage and adopt its slogans. Out went the ancient prayers of the Mass that spoke of spiritual warfare, the deceits of the Evil One, the need for ascetical violence against our fallen nature. Everything was smoothed over in recognition of the goodness of everything and everyone (if only they knew it).[4] Heavy-duty exorcisms were stripped out of the baptismal rite, where they had found a place since apostolic times in

---

ing the Papacy in a Time of Ecclesial Disintegration (Waterloo, ON: Arouca Press, 2022).

4. See Eric Sammons, *Deadly Indifference: How the Church Lost Her Mission and How We Can Reclaim It* (Manchester, NH: Crisis Publications, 2021), and my lecture "Christian Militancy in the Prayer of the Church," *OnePeterFive*, March 16, 2022, https://onepeterfive.com/christian-militancy-in-the-prayer-of-the-church.

recognition of the revealed truth that mankind after the Fall is under Satan's princedom and new citizens of heaven have to be torn away from his influence.[5] Days of fasting and abstinence were canceled out left and right; instead of renewing "ancient tradition" (as the talking heads claimed), the most genuine ancient practices were ignored or shrugged off as superstitious.[6] The only direction was downhill: dispensing, simplifying, abbreviating, abolishing.

As for self-control, the sexual morality of the Christian people worldwide—above all in the West, from which the conciliar documents and reforms emanated—is at an all-time nadir, not only because of the unforeseen intensity of the antiauthoritarian revolution of 1968 and its recurrent aftershocks, but even more because of a fundamental loss of faith in the salvific truth and liberating power of God's commandments, a loss that certainly predated 1968.

Today, in the *reductio ad absurdum* pontificate of Francis, we are reaping the putrid fruits of this loss of faith, this lack of self-control, this stripping away of all asceticism and warfare from the Christian vision of life, this foolish optimism that rippled through the Church of the 1960s and begot the demon offspring I have elsewhere called "Nietzschean Catholicism."[7] We have seen a continual compromise with the reigning forces of liberalism, a chipping away at the demands of the Gospel, a suppression of hard truths and the love of God for His own sake and above all things. The end is nothing-wor-

---

5. See my article "The Excision of Exorcisms as a Prelude to Devil-Denial," *OnePeterFive*, June 19, 2017, https://onepeterfive.com/excision-exorcisms-prelude-devil-denial. See Thomas Pink, "Vatican II and Crisis in the Theology of Baptism," in *Integralism and the Common Good: Selected Essays from* The Josias, vol. 2: *The Two Powers*, ed. Edmund Waldstein, O.Cist. (Brooklyn, NY: Angelico Press, 2022), 290–334. I dare those who think that I exaggerate the extent of the contradiction between the Catholic Magisterium and "official theology" as poured forth in the past five decades from the Vatican (including from John Paul II and Benedict XVI, *a fortiori* from Francis) to read Pink's essay. To say that it is eye-opening is a major understatement; in any case, it confirms in depth what I argue here in broad lines. See also Patricia Snow, "Satan Unbound," *First Things*, December 2022, www.firstthings.com/article/2022/12/satan-unbound.

6. See Michael P. Foley, "The Glow of the Ember Days," *Rorate Caeli*, September 23, 2015, https://rorate-caeli.blogspot.com/2008/09/glow-of-ember-days.html.

7. See Kwasniewski, *Once and Future Roman Rite*, 318–24.

ship[8]—the nihilism concentrated in the unforgettable image of a priest, later a cardinal of the Holy Roman Church, abusing a boy who happened to be the first person he baptized two weeks after his ordination.[9]

For a long time, I believed that John Paul II and Benedict XVI were fighting the good fight against this revolutionary reinterpretation of Christianity. In some ways they certainly were. But after witnessing high-profile interreligious meetings in Assisi, osculations of the Koran, book-length interviews with dialectical answers to every question, and other such indicators, I lost my enthusiasm for them *as pastors*, whatever I might admire in their philosophical or theological work (which, however you slice it, is not the primary job of a pope).[10] It was a shock to realize that these undoubtedly well-intentioned popes were swimming in a lake of postconciliar Kool-Aid rather than the millennium-spanning ocean of Tradition—the only difference being that they were strong enough to keep swimming and occasionally cried out to heaven for help, instead of drowning and sinking to the bottom like a millstone with a cardinal tied around its neck.

The last ten years are not a sudden catastrophe that came out of nowhere; they are the orange juice concentrate of the past sixty years, the last act in a tragedy that has been fitfully escalating to this point. Bergoglio is the distillate of all the worst tendencies in Roncalli, Montini, Wojtyla, and Ratzinger, without any of their redeeming qualities. Francis's predecessors were conflicted and inconsistent semi-progressives; he is a convicted Modernist. Just as political con-

---

8. To use a phrase of Thaddeus Kozinski's: "The Tradition of Nothing Worship," in *Modernity as Apocalypse: Sacred Nihilism and the Counterfeits of Logos* (Brooklyn, NY: Angelico Press, 2019), 177–86.

9. See Sharon Otterman, "Man Says Cardinal McCarrick, His 'Uncle Ted,' Sexually Abused Him for Years," *New York Times*, July 19, 2018, www.nytimes.com/2018/07/19/nyregion/mccarrick-cardinal-sexual-abuse.html.

10. The brilliance of this work does not, in any case, dispense us from the task of a careful and critical appraisal of its problematic aspects. See Maike Hickson's "The Great Influence of Joseph Ratzinger in the Revolutionary Upheaval of the Second Vatican Council," *Rorate Caeli*, December 11, 2020, https://rorate-caeli.blog spot.co m/2020/12/rorate-exclusivenew-biography-describes.html.

servatism is liberalism in slow motion,[11] so postconciliar Catholicism is modernism in slow motion. The sooner people see this, the sooner they will reject the whole failed and torturous experiment of *aggiornamento* in favor of an unequivocal embrace of the Catholic Faith in its age-old and perennially youthful liturgy, its magnificently harmonious and comprehensive doctrine, its all-demanding, life-saving morals.

Let us never forget that John Paul II and Benedict XVI were both involved in the Assisi meetings;[12] that they never questioned the rightness of the "razing of the bastions," the "turn toward the world," and the program of modernization that accompanied Vatican II; that they encouraged feminism with one hand[13] while trying to restrain it with the other; and that, above all, they appointed *and promoted* so many of the terrible bishops and cardinals under whom we are suffering today, as this chart shows (and it is far from complete):[14]

Prelate	*Ordained bishop by*	*Created cardinal by*
Theodore McCarrick	Paul VI	John Paul II
Angelo Sodano	Paul VI	John Paul II
Tarcisio Bertone	John Paul II	John Paul II
Pietro Parolin	Benedict XVI	Francis

11. See my article "Why Conservatism Is Part of the Problem, Not Part of the Solution," *OnePeterFive*, September 25, 2018, https://onepeterfive.com/why-conservatism-is-part-of-the-problem-not-part-of-the-solution.

12. For a clear and succinct explanation of why the Assisi meetings were and remain a grave scandal, see Eric Sammons, "The Legacy of Assisi," *Crisis Magazine*, October 7, 2021, www.crisismagazine.com/2021/the-legacy-of-assisi.

13. For example, by ensuring that the *Catechism* contained no reference to the headship of the husband—in spite of the fact that this is taught more frequently in the New Testament than many other doctrines of our faith—and by approving the use of female altar servers and continuing the custom of female lectors at Mass, contrary to two thousand years of universal tradition in churches of apostolic descent. See Peter Kwasniewski, *Ministers of Christ: Recovering the Roles of Clergy and Laity in an Age of Confusion* (Manchester, NH: Crisis Publications, 2021).

14. "Archbishop Viganò and Our Vale of Tears," *Unam Sanctam Catholicam*, August 29, 2018, https://unamsanctamcatholicam.blogspot.com/2018/08/archbishop-vigano-and-our-vale-of-tears.html.

Vatican II: *Requiescat in Pace*

William Levada	John Paul II	Benedict XVI
Marc Ouellet	John Paul II	John Paul II
Lorenzo Baldisseri	John Paul II	Francis
Leonardo Sandri	John Paul II	Benedict XVI
Fernando Filoni	John Paul II	Benedict XVI
Dominique Mamberti	John Paul II	Francis
Francesco Coccopalmerio	John Paul II	Benedict XVI
Giovanni Lajolo	John Paul II	Benedict XVI
Vincenzo Paglia	John Paul II	–
Edwin O'Brien	John Paul II	Benedict XVI
Renato Raffaele Martino	John Paul II	John Paul II
Donald Wuerl	John Paul II	Benedict XVI
Paul Bootkoski	John Paul II	–
John Myers	John Paul II	–
Kevin Farrell	John Paul II	Francis
Seán O'Malley	John Paul II	Benedict XVI
Oscar Rodríguez Maradiaga	John Paul II	John Paul II
Blase Cupich	John Paul II	Francis
Joseph Tobin	Benedict XVI	Francis
Robert McElroy	Benedict XVI	Francis
Edgar Peña Parra	Benedict XVI	–
John Nienstedt	John Paul II	–
Jorge Bergoglio	John Paul II	John Paul II

To this chart may be added the following names:

• Cardinal Karl Lehmann (1936–2018), made a bishop by John Paul II in 1983 and created a cardinal by the same in 2001;

• Cardinal Carlo Maria Martini (1927–2012), made an archbishop by John Paul II in 1979 and a created a cardinal by the same in 1983;

• Cardinal Walter Kasper (b. 1933), made a bishop by John Paul II in 1989 and made a cardinal by the same in 2001;

• Cardinal Cormac Murphy-O'Connor (1932–2017), made a bishop by Paul VI (1977) and created cardinal by John Paul II in 2001.

Truly, one wishes to know how it happened that, although John Paul II had ousted the Saint Gallen Group around 1993 from their power positions in the Council of the Bishops' Conference of Europe (CCEE), he then made them all cardinals in the same year! It has all the marks of a deal brokered in secret.[15]

Consequently, we cannot lay *all* the blame at the feet of Francis; he is grimly reaping what his predecessors have sown, even while he is tearing down much of what they built. In the end, there are two reasons we had the cardinals who voted for Bergoglio: Wojtyla and Ratzinger. More generally, they are the reason we have a worldwide episcopacy made up of a tiny minority of traditional bishops (by which I mean bishops who believe, preach, teach, and enforce the Catholic faith as taught, *inter alia*, by the Council of Trent) and a huge majority of ferocious liberals, toothless conservatives, and pencil-pushing bureaucrats. If John Paul II had spent far less time globetrotting and writing massive, dense, and now mostly forgotten encyclicals (with *Veritatis Splendor* and *Ecclesia de Eucharistia* as glowing exceptions) and far more time on his single most important duty, that of vetting and choosing bishops of proven doctrinal orthodoxy, moral probity, and commitment to the sacred liturgy— men without the slightest hint of liberalism or laxity—the Church would be in a dramatically different and better place today.[16] The same could be said of the beloved but largely ineffectual professor-turned-pontiff Benedict XVI. That he had a retiring personality turned from a forgivable quirk into a nightmare on February 11, 2013.

These two popes also knew—as we now see in ever greater detail—about wicked behavior in high places, yet seldom took deci-

---

15. See Julia Meloni, *The St. Gallen Mafia: Exposing the Secret Reformist Group Within the Church* (Gastonia, NC: TAN Books, 2021).

16. See the appendix of *Are Canonizations Infallible? Revisiting a Disputed Question*, ed. Peter A. Kwasniewski (Waterloo, ON: Arouca Press, 2021), for Prospero Lambertini's considerations on the essential criteria for papal sanctity, on which I pattern my statements here.

sive and severe measures to uproot it. Bergoglio celebrates the unnatural vice that his predecessors tolerated. Bergoglio shamelessly promotes those enemies of Catholicism whom his predecessors were too afraid to fight.

Can we say, at least, that practicing and believing Catholics *generally* have been awakened from their dogmatic slumber?

Would that it were so. The capacity of the human mind to ignore reality even when it is crashing around one's head is all too real—as real as the capacity for ideology to blind the eye and deafen the ear. But for those with eyes to see and ears to hear, the truth has emerged into broad daylight: the Catholic faith as our forefathers believed and lived it, the Catholic faith as a vast cloud of witnesses knew it and loved it, *this Catholic faith is something utterly different from what is being peddled by the Vatican today.* What the new regime offers is ephemeral, fragile, and self-contradictory, held together only by force. The alternative is equally clear: the complex but internally consistent religion taught by the Fathers and Doctors of the Church; savored by monks and mystics; authoritatively proclaimed by the great councils; unanimously codified in hundreds of catechisms; and, above all, luminously, exultantly embodied in the great liturgical rites of East and West, the common heritage of all orthodox Christians who worship the thrice-holy Trinity in an unbroken tradition.

That is Catholicism. Nothing else. Do not look for it where it cannot be found. Do not strain or break your neck trying to find a way to look at the novelties as if they were tradition, for it cannot be done. Do not strain the gnat while swallowing the camel. Hearken again to the one true Faith that missionized the globe in the *Old Evangelization.*

What will it take to free every last Catholic from the last illusions about the supposed "new springtime" of Vatican II? I do not know. It may be that death alone will conquer these illusions, but there are certainly many signs that the charm—or perhaps more accurately, the mirage—is vanishing, as many find their way back to the divine religion of Christ.

II

Fr. Dwight Longenecker is a fine writer. No one expresses a certain point of view better than he does. I'm not sure how to characterize it exactly; it might be described as a *via-media*-at-all-costs,[17] the straight road that seems to veer neither to the left nor to the right. He is determined to place himself between the extremes of the "trendies" and the "traddies" so that, in company with a remnant including at least George Weigel, he will emerge from this crisis not tarred and feathered as a progressive or bedecked with bays and rosemary as a traditionalist, but stolidly, if lonesomely, centrist.

Such thoughts are prompted by an article of his entitled "What Shall We Do about Vatican II?,"[18] which takes the form of a paean to Cardinal Sarah's book, *The Day Is Now Far Spent*. Bear with me, then, as I digress for a moment about this book.

The Day Is Now Far Spent has a lot of good material in it. How could it not? Cardinal Sarah is a keen-sighted observer of the modern West, its accelerating apostasy and diabolical decomposition. He is a man who has a thing or two to say about the grave problems facing the Church. What is very strange, however, is what Cardinal Sarah does *not* see—or is not willing to admit, either to himself or perhaps to his readership. For example, the dedication of his book reads, in part, as follows: "For Benedict XVI, peerless architect of the rebuilding of the Church. For Francis, faithful and devoted son of St. Ignatius."

A priest friend of mine, who like me is an admirer of Sarah's previous books, *God or Nothing* and *The Power of Silence*, told me that when he saw this dedication, he wanted to chuck the book across the room. He summed up his reaction: "Benedict, the shepherd who fled for fear of the wolves? *He's* the peerless architect of the Church's rebuilding? That's like saying a father who abandons his

---

17. See "Can We Love Tradition Too Much?" in Peter Kwasniewski, *Reclaiming Our Roman Catholic Birthright: The Genius and Timeliness of the Traditional Latin Mass* (Brooklyn, NY: Angelico Press, 2020), 181–92.

18. First published at Fr. Longenecker's blog *Standing on My Head* on November 19, 2019, https://dwightlongenecker.com/what-shall-we-do-about-vatican-two.

children to an abusive stepfather is the peerless architect of his family's success. And Francis, a faithful and devoted son of St. Ignatius? That saint must be rolling in his grave about the modern Jesuits and *this* Jesuit above all, who says and does the opposite of everything Ignatius lived and died for." In a similar albeit milder vein, Jeff Mirus wrote in his withering review:

> If the dilemma [of Catholics today] really does have Pope Francis at its center (and I do not see how any reasonable observer can doubt this), I have to say that the details of Cardinal Sarah's solution are unworkable. For Cardinal Sarah always goes out of his way to indicate not only that he is not opposed to Pope Francis in any way but that in everything he writes he is echoing the Holy Father's themes. Believe me, I get this; I understand why he chooses this path; but in the end, he pushes it too far and it just will not do.
>
> It is true, of course, that Cardinal Sarah does not in any canonical or obediential sense "oppose the Pope"—a point which he makes with appalling sloppiness from time to time.... And it is true that Cardinal Sarah works hard at creating the illusion that he is following up lines of thought proposed by Pope Francis himself.... But in fact, the grand alliance of what we might call "The Friends of Pope Francis" constantly tries to bring against Cardinal Sarah this charge of opposition to the Pope, precisely because it is so obvious that Sarah's constant recommendations are seriously at odds with much of what Pope Francis says.
>
> What is clear to everyone in this is that Cardinal Sarah has tried mightily to find a few good quotes from Pope Francis—and, after all, there are many to be found if a student can survive the avalanche of intellectual and spiritual confusion long enough to dig them out—so that he can maintain the fictional aspect of his method throughout the book.[19]

I am reminded of an ad I saw for the Augustine Institute, in which a course on moral theology was named "Who am I to judge?" and—cleverly (?)—Pope Francis was trotted out with a quotation

19. Jeff Mirus, "Robert Cardinal Sarah's dilemma, and our own," *Catholic Culture*, October 23, 2019, www.catholicculture.org/commentary/robert-cardinal-sara hs-dilemma-and-our-own.

opposed to relativism. As if to say… as if to say *what*, exactly? That he's really and truly *on our side*, on the side of Catholic tradition, Catholic theology, Catholic life? Stringing up those good quotes like so many blinking Christmas lights will not chase away the cavernous darkness.

Fr. Longenecker praises Cardinal Sarah for following and testifying to the *via media* between the trendies who got drunk off the spirits of Vatican II and the teetotaling traddies who will not touch the stuff. The viamedians will locate, with determination, the (more or less) traditional-sounding quotes from Vatican II and say: "See? I told you so. It's not all bad! Now we can forget our troubles with a big bowl of ice cream." It's important, in any case, not to look too closely into the history of the Council and the shaping of its documents; the manifold lines of influence connecting *nouvelle théologie* and *ressourcement* with Modernism; the way Paul VI and his episcopal and curial appointments adopted a line that conflicted with Catholic beliefs and instincts on point after point; and above all, the final stages of the liturgical reform (ca. 1963–1974),[20] which—in its artisanal blend of *faux*-ancient, quasi-Eastern, and *de novo* sources, "active participation," options galore, vernacular, and new music—resembles nothing Roman or Catholic from all the centuries of the Church's history and enjoys validity in a vacuum.[21] Those who broach such issues are not engaged with in a serious way, but are written off as "radical Catholic reactionaries" whom everyone should be strong-armed—or Armstronged?—to avoid like the plague. I suppose that's one way to deal with uncomfortable truths, but it's not recommended for those who are seeking the real causes of today's crisis.

Like George Weigel, who pontificates that "nostalgia for an imaginary past is not a reliable guide to the future,"[22] Fr. Longenecker

---

20. See my article "What Bugnini Was Thinking When He Destroyed the Catholic Mass," *OnePeterFive*, February 5, 2019, https://onepeterfive.com/bugnini-destroyed-mass.

21. See Kwasniewski, *Once and Future Roman Rite*, 33–77 and 145–77.

22. "The Reformed Liturgy, Fifty Years Later," *First Things*, November 27, 2019, www.firstthings.com/web-exclusives/2019/11/the-reformed-liturgy-50-years-later.

expresses his concern about those who "do" beautiful Tridentine liturgies: "If one is not careful it all becomes no more than an exercise in nostalgia and no more authentic than Cinderella's castle at Disneyland."

I wish someone would explain to the Longeneckers and Weigels of the world that whatever else is going on, nostalgia plays no role in it. Most of the people in a modern Latin Mass congregation were born well after Vatican II and have not the slightest clue what things were like beforehand, nor do they particularly care. They are not hankering for a lost culture or seeking to reconstruct a lost world. Rather, they desire a proper Catholic culture *here and now*, which begins with the solemn, formal, objective, beautiful divine cult we call the sacred liturgy, which we *do* inherit from many centuries of faith—but we live it and we love it *now*. Moreover, the elderly who join us for the traditional Mass are well aware that much of what we are doing after *Summorum Pontificum* is better than what they saw as children—and they are grateful for it. Generally speaking, the Low Masses are more reverently recited; the High Masses, even Solemn High Masses, are more frequent, better attended, and more resplendent.

The phenomenon of nostalgia is found, rather, among those who wish they could recover the glory days of John Paul II, when it seemed the Church was riding high (as if we might, just might, recover at last from the postconciliar tailspin); among Boomers, for whom Marty Haugen's music "hath charms to soothe a savage breast, to soften rocks, or bend a knotted oak"; and among elderly churchmen who long for the halcyon days of Vatican II. Trads are clearsighted, energetic, and future-looking people. They are too busy discerning vocations, managing a pewful of children, singing in chant scholas, or cooking for potlucks after Rorate Masses to have time for lollygagging in the lanes of an inaccessible memory. It's the ones hugging their *Breaking Bread* hymnals or their "JP II We Love You" teddy bears who are the misty-eyed sentimentalists.

Along these lines, Fr. Longenecker still believes in the "hermeneutic of continuity" between the premodern Church and the Church of Vatican II. This hermeneutic died when Pope Benedict resigned. That act of abandoning the flock to the wolves symbolized the practical and theoretical abandonment of this vision of harmony ("if only we could just *read* what the sixteen documents *actually say!*") and its replacement by the more sober realization that the Council chose accommodation to the mind and modes of modernity over clear continuity with tradition.[23] We are now reaping the poisonous fruits of that choice.

We can see, moreover, the full magnitude of the evils that remained in the Church in spite of, and at times *because of*, John Paul II and Benedict XVI. Despite their indubitably great qualities, both of these popes spent too much time traveling, professorializing, and praying for peace with non-Catholics, and too little time mucking out the stables, replenishing the hired hands, and rebuilding the fallen structures of the Church. Were it not for their misplaced priorities, we would not be suffering under the twin burdens of an entrenched clerico-homosexual culture and a rigid adherence to soft modernism at all levels and in all areas.[24]

At one point Fr. Longenecker says, concerning the Council's "opening to the world" and "a spirituality for all with open doors to all": "I am grateful for the spirit of openness, but also grateful for the spirit of *resourcement* [*sic*]—going back to the roots." The first difficulty here is that it is not the business of the Church to open herself to the world. Even *after* the Lord's Incarnation, Death, and Resurrection decisively changed fallen man's opportunities for salvation, the Lord's three favored apostles Peter, James, and John still took pains to tell us that, once we have "escaped from the corruption that is in that world" (2 Pt 1:4), we should "love not the world, nor the things which are in the world" (1 Jn. 2:15), since "whosoever will be a friend of this world becometh an enemy of God" (Jas. 4:4). All of this St. Paul pithily endorses: "Be not conformed to this world" (Rom. 12:2). The second difficulty lies in the assertion that

---

23. See "The Failure of Todaying," in Kwasniewski, *Reclaiming Our Roman Catholic Birthright*, 213–21.

24. See "No Matter How Bad You Think the Corruption Is, It's Worse," in Kwasniewski, *Road from Hyperpapalism to Catholicism*, vol. 1, 134–40, and "Pius X to Francis: From Modernism Expelled to Modernism Enthroned," *Road from Hyperpapalism to Catholicism*, vol. 2, 283–306.

Vatican II sought to reconnect us with our heritage, our "sources." This claim is more than questionable; it is Big Baloney. If the churchmen in charge had been really interested in *ressourcement* or returning to the roots, they would have preserved our traditional liturgy, which connects us to the Church of every age, instead of inventing a hybrid antiquarian-ultramodern liturgy for Modern Man.™ The architects of the Council, who, lucky for us, wrote and spoke freely about their intentions, were trying rather to domesticate the Modernism of the nineteenth and early twentieth centuries, to make it mainstream and acceptable—the "Trojan Horse" about which Dietrich von Hildebrand perceptively spoke. It was above all the philosophers, sociologists, and anthropologists who saw the magnitude of the change, because they are accustomed to thinking carefully about phenomena, causality, patterns, and movements.

Fr. Longenecker may well be right that Vatican II "brought him into the Church." But God can and frequently does write straight with crooked lines. He awakened my love for church music in a parish covered with carpet and extraordinary ministers. He brought me to a more serious faith through the charismatic renewal and later by the Novus Ordo in Latin, which are classic waystations: as with a first girlfriend, or a first job out of college, it's not the place one usually ends up. One's faith matures; one sees that what used to satisfy begins to look shallow, brittle, awkward, forced. The Lord led me beyond these waystations into full-blooded Catholic thought, culture, and worship. "Loyalty to tradition, love of traditional liturgy and devotions, and the depth of traditional Catholic spirituality"—in Fr. Longenecker's eloquent words—are not particularly characteristic of Vatican II or any phase of its implementation. Those who want to find them and keep them are going to need to look elsewhere.

As an historical event, Vatican II recedes further and further into the past—and into irrelevance. I recall an author saying, some years ago in *First Things*, that for his students in the college classroom "Vatican II" evoked neither more nor less than "Chalcedon" or "Ephesus." These words and their nominal definitions all had to be chiseled with equal effort into the blank slates, not to say blank stares.

In terms of its theological or spiritual contributions, whether in the proclamation of definitions and anathemas or in the unleashing of edifying energies, Vatican II is looking more and more like the most fussed over and the most negligible council in the Church's history. If it disappeared into thin air, what of lasting value would we actually *lose*? The vocation of the laity? That was already there in Leo XIII's *Sapientiae Christianae*, in the ranks of Catholic Action, in ubiquitous Confraternities and Third Orders, in vibrant cultural-intellectual currents that made Catholicism appealing to artists and intellectuals throughout the twentieth century. A renewed consciousness of priesthood and episcopacy? The Fathers of the Church and earlier popes had wisely discoursed on these matters, with better penetration and realism. How the Catholic Church relates to other Christian bodies and non-Christian religions, or the proper manner of conceiving and structuring Church-State relations? One cannot so much as mention ecumenism, interreligious dialogue, and political theology without wincing in embarrassment or alarm at the distortions they have experienced in the Council's name; only recently, for example, has the rich vein of integralism been rediscovered.[25] Or, if the Council disappeared, would we lose something of lasting value when it comes to the way we ought to "worship God in spirit and in truth" in the sacred liturgy? Considering that increasing numbers of Catholics have either abandoned going to church for the "renewed rites" or seek refuge in the marginalized traditional Latin Mass, the question rather answers itself.

When we consider the sheer magnitude of positive, constructive, tradition-guarding reform inaugurated and guided for centuries by the Council of Trent, we are justified in concluding that Vatican II, in stark contrast, was a monumental failure. Church councils of the past always sought to bring clarity to debated questions, refine the expression of doctrine, bear witness to the fullness of the Faith, and fearlessly condemn errors. In doing these things, they were *truly*

---

25. See the two anthologies published by Angelico Press under the title *Integralism and the Common Good: Selected Essays from* The Josias.

pastoral. The councils did not indulge in ambiguity, sow obscurity, backtrack, sidestep, enthrone a nebulous pastorality as the primary concern, or refrain from condemnation due to a sentimental carica-ture of mercy—or, in the case of Communism, due to secretive deals with Soviet collaborators among the Russian Orthodox. This is why Vatican II is the great exception and the great dead end. The Council Is Now Far Spent.

Fr. Longenecker concludes his article by saying Cardinal Sarah "has the final word." If that is true, we are sorry folks, indeed, for he is merely repeating the same stale advice that conservatives have been giving ineffectually and unsuccessfully for fifty years: "Just read the documents *more carefully* and you will see…" As a matter of fact, let's draw a contrast between Cardinal Sarah and another bishop who *is* reading the Council carefully, Bishop Athanasius Schneider. Bishop Schneider's book-length interview *Christus Vin-cit: Christ's Triumph over the Darkness of the Age*, which appeared at about the same time as the cardinal's, takes prizes in all categories: in its moving personal stories, in its remarkable range of topics, in its depth and clarity of argumentation, in its honest grappling with our situation. Bishop Schneider, a far more reliable and realistic guide than Cardinal Sarah, is not afraid to point out serious flaws not only in the way the Council's texts have been wielded, but in those texts themselves.

To Fr. Longenecker's question, then—"What shall we do about Vatican II?"—I suggest we leave it alone, leave it behind, leave it in peace, along with Lyons I, Lateran V, and other councils you've never heard of, and turn our minds and hands to better things ahead: reaffirming and rekindling the one, holy, catholic, and apos-tolic religion that predated it and still endures six decades later. By God's grace, neither the Faith nor its liturgical expression, neither the *lex credendi* nor the *lex orandi*, can be altogether obliterated from the face of the Earth.

If I might change the conversation, I would say a more pressing question is: "What shall we do about Vatican I?" December 8, 2019 marked the 150th anniversary of the opening of a council that would forever change the way Catholics perceived and interacted with the papacy. In many ways, we are more threatened today by "the spirit of

Vatican I"—a runaway hyperpapalism capable of leveling centuries of tradition—which will take a mighty exorcism to drive away.[26]

III

Is the recent "attack" on Vatican II a "crisis moment" for traditionalists, as some have claimed? Are we turning against a legitimate and laudable Council instead of rightly directing our ire at the inept leadership that has followed in its wake and betrayed its vital truths? That has been the line of conservatives for a long time: a "hermeneutic of continuity" combined with strong criticism of episcopal and clerical brigandage. The implausibility of this approach is demonstrated by, among other signs, the infinitesimal success that conservatives have had in reversing the disastrous "reforms," trends, habits, and institutions established, with papal approbation or toleration, in the wake of and in the name of the last council.

What Archbishop Viganò has said in recent years about the Council with a forthrightness unusual in today's prelates is but a new installment in a longstanding critique offered by Catholic traditionalists from Michael Davies to Romano Amerio, Roberto de Mattei to Henry Sire. We have watched bishops, episcopal conferences, cardinals, and popes construct a "new paradigm," piece by piece, for more than half a century—a "new" Catholic faith that at best only partially overlaps with and at worst downright contradicts the traditional Catholic faith as we find it expressed in the Church Fathers and Doctors, the earlier councils, and hundreds of traditional catechisms,[27] not to mention the old Latin liturgical rites that were suppressed and replaced with radically different ones. So enormous a chasm gapes between the old Faith and its new version that we cannot refrain from asking about the role played by the Second Vatican Ecumenical Council in the unfolding of a modernist story that has its beginning in the late nineteenth century and its denoue-

---

26. See Kwasniewski, *Road from Hyperpapalism to Catholicism*, vol. 1, 1–27, 107–11, and 120–26. See also John P. Joy, *Disputed Questions on Papal Infallibility* (Lincoln, NE: Os Justi Press, 2022).

27. See "Traditional Catholic Catechisms," *Whispers of Restoration*, www.whispersofrestoration.com/traditional-catechisms, and the Tradivox project published by Sophia Institute Press, https://www.tradivox.com.

ment in the present. The line from Loisy, Tyrrell, and Hügel[28] to Küng, Teilhard, and (young) Ratzinger[29] to Kasper, Bergoglio, and Tagle[30] is straight enough when one starts connecting the dots. This is not to say there are not interesting and important differences among these men. But they share principles that would have been branded as dubious, dangerous, or heretical by *any* of the great confessors and theologians, from Augustine and Chrysostom to Aquinas and Bellarmine.

We have to abandon once and for all the naïveté of thinking that the only thing that matters about Vatican II are its promulgated texts. No. In this case, progressives and traditionalists are right to insist that the *event* matters as much as the texts.[31] The vagueness of purpose for which the Council was convened; the manipulative way

28. In addition to my lecture "Pius X to Francis: From Modernism Expelled to Modernism Enthroned," see Matthew Karmel, "A Crisis of Meaning: Sacred Scripture and the Rise of Modernism (Pt. I)," *OnePeterFive*, May 26, 2016, https://onepeterfive.com/crisis-meaning-sacred-scripture-rise-modernism-pt-ii; Charles Coulombe, "Heretic of the Week: George Tyrrell," *Catholic Herald*, January 10, 2019, https://catholicherald.co.uk/heretic-of-the-week-george-tyrrell; Philip Trower, "The First Modernism," in *The Church Learned and the Revolt of the Scholars* (The Wanderer Press, 1979), excerpt published at *Catholic Culture*, undated, www.catholicculture.org/culture/library/view.cfm?recnum=3746.

29. See Jason Berry, "Hans Küng, influential Catholic dissident, confronts his own mortality," *The World*, December 19, 2013, www.pri.org/stories/2013-12-19/hans-k-ng-influential-catholic-dissident-confronts-his-own-mortality; Peter Kwasniewski, "Teilhard de Chardin: Model of Ambiguity for a Future Pope," *OnePeterFive*, January 16, 2019, https://onepeterfive.com/teilhard-chardin-ambiguity-pope; John Wilkins, "Ratzinger at Vatican II: A Pope Who Can & Cannot Change," *Commonweal*, May 31, 2010, www.commonwealmagazine.org/ratzinger-vatican-ii.

30. See Thomas Heinrich Stark, "German Idealism and Cardinal Kasper's Theological Project," *Catholic World Report*, June 9, 2015, www.catholicworldreport.com/2015/06/09/german-idealism-and-cardinal-kaspers-theological-project; Leonardo de Chirico, "The Intellectual Journey of J.M. Bergoglio, Now Pope Francis," *Vatican Files*, April 1, 2018, https://evangelicalfocus.com/vatican-files/3392/the-intellectual-journey-of-jm-bergoglio-now-pope-francis; John L. Allen Jr., "In Tagle, Pope strengthens his Vatican hand and sets up possible successor," *Crux*, December 11, 2019, https://cruxnow.com/news-analysis/2019/12/in-tagle-pope-strengthens-his-vatican-hand-and-sets-up-possible-successor.

31. For a most convincing presentation, see Roberto de Mattei's *The Second Vatican Council—An Unwritten Story*.

it was conducted; the consistently liberal way in which it was implemented (or allowed to be implemented), with barely a whimper from the world's episcopacy—none of this is irrelevant to interpreting the meaning and significance of the Council texts, which themselves exhibit novel genres and dangerous ambiguities, not to mention passages that have all the traits of flat-out error, such as the teaching on Muslims and Christians "adoring" the same God, of which Bishop Schneider gives a devastating critique in *Christus Vincit*.[32] It is surprising that, at this late stage, there would still be defenders of the Council documents, when it is clear that they have lent and still lend themselves exquisitely to the goal of the Church's supine secularization, her modernization via detachment from her history and inheritance. Even if the documents' content were unobjectionable, their verbosity, complexity, and mingling of obvious truths with head-scratching ideas furnished the perfect pretext for the revolution. This revolution is now melted into these texts, fused with them like metal pieces passed through a superheated oven.

Thus, the very act of quoting Vatican II has become a signal that one wishes to align with all that has been done by the popes—yes, by the *popes*—in its name. At the forefront is the liturgical destruction, but examples could be multiplied *ad nauseam*: consider such dismal moments as the aforementioned Assisi interreligious gatherings, the logic of which John Paul II defended exclusively in terms of a string of quotations from Vatican II. The pontificate of Francis has merely stepped on the accelerator. Always it is Vatican II that is trotted out to explain or justify every deviation and departure from the historic dogmatic faith. Is all this purely coincidental—a series of remarkably unfortunate interpretations and wayward judgments that an honest reading of the texts could dispel, like the sun blazing through the rainclouds?

"But aren't there good things in the documents?" many rush to say.

I have studied and taught the documents of the Council, some of

---

32. For a synopsis, see Maike Hickson, "Bishop Schneider: Catholics and Muslims Share No Common Faith in God, No Common Adoration," *LifeSiteNews*, June 8, 2020, www.lifesitenews.com/blogs/bishop-schneider-catholics-and-muslims-share-no-common-faith-in-god-no-common-adoration.

them numerous times. I know them well. Since I am a "Great Books" devotee and have always taught for Great Books schools, my theology courses would typically begin with Scripture and the Fathers, then go into the scholastics (especially St. Thomas) and finish up with magisterial texts: papal encyclicals and conciliar documents. I will admit that I often felt a sinking of the heart when the course, after luxuriating in the best witnesses of our tradition, reached a Vatican II document such as *Lumen Gentium, Sacrosanctum Concilium, Dignitatis Humanae, Unitatis Redintegratio, Nostra Aetate,* or *Gaudium et Spes.* Of course—of course!—they have much that is beautiful and orthodox in them: they could never have gotten the requisite number of votes had they been flagrantly opposed to Catholic teaching. However, they are sprawling, unwieldy, inconsistent committee products that needlessly complicate many subjects and lack the crystalline clarity a council is supposed to work hard to achieve. All you have to do is look at the documents of Trent or the first seven Ecumenical Councils to see brilliant examples of this tightly constructed style, which cut off heresy at every possible point to the extent the council fathers were capable of doing at that particular juncture.[33] And then there are the sentences in Vatican II—not a few of them—at which ones stops and says: "Am I really seeing these words on the page in front of me? What a [fill in as needed: messy; problematic; proximate-to-error; erroneous] thing to say."[34]

I used to hold, with conservatives, that we should "take what's good in the Council and leave behind the rest." The danger in this approach is well expressed by Pope Leo XIII:

---

33. It is worthy of note that John XXIII had appointed preparatory commissions that produced short, tight, clear documents for the upcoming council to work with—and then allowed the liberal or "Rhine" faction of Council Fathers to chuck out these drafts and replace them with new ones. The only exception was *Sacrosanctum Concilium*, Bugnini's project, which sailed through without much trouble. See Paolo Pasqualucci, *The Parallel Council: The Anomalous Beginning of the Second Vatican Council* (Fort Collins, CO: Gondolin Press, 2018).

34. It's not just a matter of poor translations; the first translations were generally good, while later translations tended to dumb down the texts.

The Arians, the Montanists, the Novatians, the Quartodecimans, the Eutychians, certainly did not reject all Catholic doctrine: they abandoned only a certain portion of it. Still who does not know that they were declared heretics and banished from the bosom of the Church? In like manner were condemned all authors of heretical tenets who followed them in subsequent ages. "There can be nothing more dangerous than those heretics who admit nearly the whole cycle of doctrine, and yet by one word, as with a drop of poison, infect the real and simple faith taught by our Lord and handed down by Apostolic tradition" (*Tract. de Fide Orthodoxa contra Arianos*).[35]

In other words: it is the mixture, the jumble, of sublime, great, good, indifferent, bad, generic, ambiguous, problematic, erroneous, and all of it at enormous length, that makes Vatican II uniquely deserving of repudiation.[36]

"Weren't there always problems after Church councils?" replies the entrenched apologist.

Yes, without a doubt: Church councils have nearly always been followed by controversy to a greater or lesser degree. Yet these difficulties were usually *in spite of*, not *because of*, the nature and content of the documents. St. Athanasius could appeal again and again to Nicaea as to a battle ensign, because its teaching was succinct and rock-solid, conforming to the tradition of prayer known to every layman.[37] The popes after the Council of Trent could appeal again and again to its canons and decrees because the teaching was succinct and rock-solid. While Trent produced a large number of documents over the course of the nearly two decades during which the

---

35. Leo XIII, Encyclical Letter on the Unity of the Church *Satis Cognitum*, June 29, 1896, n. 9.

36. As Cardinal Walter Kasper admitted in an article published in *L'Osservatore Romano* on April 12, 2013: "In many places, [the Council Fathers] had to find compromise formulas, in which, often, the positions of the majority are located immediately next to those of the minority, designed to delimit them. Thus, the conciliar texts themselves have a huge potential for conflict, opening the door to a selective reception in either direction."

37. Note, with Nicaea, that it was the familiar *lex orandi* that sustained the council's *lex credendi*—not the bizarre reversal whereby a council, Vatican II, is dictating the need to change the *lex orandi*!

sessions took place (1545–1563), each document is a marvel of clarity, with not a wasted word. Like earlier councils, the documents of Trent also admirably distinguish sharply between dogmatic matters and disciplinary ones. First, the truth, explained, defined, and defended against opposing errors; then, in second place, the plethora of practical or prudential measures that need to be taken, and which, of their nature, are not guaranteed infallibility, much less immutability. Such a distinction of levels would have been enormously helpful in the Second Vatican Council's documents as well, as it would have prevented time-bound, prudential, mutable, fallible proposals (like the bulk of *Sacrosanctum Concilium*) from being elevated into unquestioned tenets of faith to which we must cling with blind fervor even when their failure is evident.

At the very least, the Vatican II documents failed miserably in facilitating the Council's purpose as explained by Pope John XXIII. He said in 1962 that he wanted a more accessible presentation of the faith for Modern Man.™ By 1965, it had become painfully obvious that the sixteen documents would never be something you could just gather into a book and hand out to every layman or inquirer. One might say the Council fell between two stools: it produced neither an accessible point of entry for the modern world nor a succinct "plan of engagement" for pastors and theologians to rely upon. What *did* it accomplish? A huge amount of paperwork, a lot of windy prose, and a winky nudge: "Adapt to the modern world, boys!" (Or, if you *don't*, get in trouble with—to borrow a phrase from Hobbes—"the irresistible power of the mortal god" in Rome, as Archbishop Lefebvre quickly discovered.)

This is why the last council is absolutely irrecoverable. If the project of modernization has resulted in a massive loss of Catholic identity, even of basic doctrinal competence and morals, the way forward is to pay one's last respects to the great symbol of that project and see it buried. As Martin Mosebach says, true "reform" always means a *return to form*—that is, a return to stricter discipline, clearer doctrine, fuller worship. It does not and cannot mean the opposite.

Is there *anything* of the substance of the faith, or anything of indisputable benefit, that we would lose were we to bid the last council goodbye and never hear its name mentioned again? The Catholic Tradition already has within itself immense (and, especially today, largely untapped) resources for dealing with every vexing question we face in today's world. Now, almost a quarter of the way into a different century, we are at a very different place, and the tools we need are not those of the 1960s.

"What, then, can be done in the future?"

Ever since Archbishop Viganò's letter of June 9, 2020 and his subsequent writing on the subject, people have been discussing what it might mean to "annul" the Second Vatican Council.[38] I see three theoretical possibilities for a future pope:

1. He could publish a new *Syllabus of Errors* (as Bishop Schneider proposed in 2010[39]) that identifies and condemns common errors associated with Vatican II while not attributing them explicitly to Vatican II: "If anyone says XYZ, let him be anathema." This would leave open the degree to which the Council documents actually contain the errors; it would, however, close the door to many popular "readings" of the Council.

2. He could declare that, in looking back over the past half-century, we can see that the Council documents, on account of their ambiguities and difficulties, have caused more harm than good in the life of the Church and should, in the future, no longer be referenced as authoritative in theological discussion. The Council should be treated as a historic event whose relevance has passed. Again, this stance would not need to assert that the documents are in error; rather, it would acknowledge that the Council has shown itself to be "more trouble than it's worth." Its day is far spent.

---

38. Many of these writings are contained in *A Voice in the Wilderness: Archbishop Carlo Maria Viganò on the Church, America, and the World*, ed. Brian M. McCall (Brooklyn, NY: Angelico Press, 2021). While I admire the archbishop for his "house-cleaning" intervention on the McCarrick affair and agree with much else he has written on the Council and the liturgy, in recent times his work has taken such strange turns, especially after the start of the Russian-Ukraine conflict, that I can no longer endorse it.

39. See "Proposals for a Correct Reading of the Second Vatican Council," *EWTN*, undated, www.ewtn.com/catholicism/library/proposals-for-a-correct-reading-of-the-second-vatican-council-3837.

3. He could specifically "disown" or set aside certain documents or parts of documents, even as parts of the Council of Constance were never recognized or were repudiated.

The second and third possibilities stem from a recognition that the Council took the form, unique among all Ecumenical Councils in the history of the Church, of being "pastoral" in purpose and nature, according to both John XXIII and Paul VI; this would make its setting aside relatively easy. To the objection that it still, perforce, concerns matters of faith and morals, I would reply that the bishops never defined anything and never anathematized anything. Even the "dogmatic constitutions" establish no dogma but serve as expositions, more or less successful, of dogmas already established. It is a curiously expository and catechetical council, which settles almost nothing and unsettles a great deal.

Whenever and however a future pope or council deals with this thoroughly entrenched mess, our task as Catholics remains what it has always been: to hold fast to the faith of our fathers in its normative, trustworthy expressions, namely, the *lex orandi* of the traditional liturgical rites of East and West, the *lex credendi* of the approved Creeds and the consistent witness of the infallible universal ordinary Magisterium, and the *lex vivendi* shown to us by the saints canonized over the centuries, before the era of confusion set in. This is enough, and more than enough.

IV

It is certainly a "sign of the times" to see so many discussions today of the Second Vatican Council, most of which are much more realistic in their assessment of its possible defects than has ever been the case in decades past when it was obligatory to celebrate the Council as a veritable new Pentecost, or at the very least as a moment of rectifying the problems bequeathed by four centuries of Tridentine Catholicism. We have Archbishop Viganò to thank for reigniting a discussion that one might characterize as "better late than never."

Unfortunately, many of the responses published since Viganò's "Vatican II Marked the Beginning of a False, Parallel Church" seem motivated by a desire to "save ecclesial face." George Weigel takes refuge in benign generalities and Wojtylan hero worship.[40] Adam De Ville appeals to Volkanology to write off critiques of the Council as time-collapsing "chosen trauma."[41] Bishop Barron provides tidy sound-bite answers to massive questions.[42] John Cavadini expresses sympathy with Viganò but, after cataloguing all the wonderful things he finds in the Council, simply takes refuge in Benedict XVI's assertion that it was not the Council documents at fault, but their one-sided application or development by postconciliar theologians[43]—not acknowledging that the ones who applied or developed them were the same theologians who had drafted or influenced the conciliar documents to begin with and who knew precisely what novelties and ambiguities had been lodged in them. To my mind, only Anthony Esolen and Hubert Windisch have shown that they grasped Viganò's points: for Esolen, "the Council's time in history has passed," and it needs to be "de-throned,"[44] while for Windisch, the roots of the crisis are clearly to be seen in the "repositioning" of the Church vis-à-vis the world that was the central concern of the Council's pastoral strategy.[45]

A more sophisticated defense of Vatican II was mounted by Fr. Thomas G. Weinandy, OFM Cap. in an essay entitled "Vatican II and

---

40. "The Next Pope and Vatican II," *First Things*, July 15, 2020, www.firstthings.com/web-exclusives/2020/07/the-next-pope-and-vatican-ii.

41. "Vatican II as 'chosen trauma' and 'chosen glory,'" *Catholic World Report*, July 23, 2020, www.catholicworldreport.com/2020/07/23/vatican-ii-as-chosen-trauma-and-chosen-glory.

42. See "Bishop Barron on Vatican II," *YouTube*, July 13, 2020, https://tinyurl.com/579kfy75.

43. "Was Vatican II a Bad Seed?" *Church Life Journal*, July 29, 2020, https://churchlifejournal.nd.edu/articles/is-vatican-ii-bad-seed; also published as Letter #15 of *The Moynihan Letters* at *Inside the Vatican*, July 28, 2020.

44. "De-throning Vatican II: The Council's time in history has passed," Letter #13 of *The Moynihan Letters* at *Inside the Vatican*, July 22, 2020, https://insidethevatican.com/magazine/de-throning-vatican-ii.

45. "Could Roots of Vatican II Council Result in a Church That Leaves God Behind?" *LifeSiteNews*, July 27, 2020, www.lifesitenews.com/blogs/could-roots-of-vatican-ii-council-result-in-a-church-that-leaves-god-behind. Also worth reading is Fr. Serafino M. Lanzetta's essay "Vatican II and the Calvary of the Church," *Catholic Family News*, August 3, 2020, https://catholicfamilynews.com/blog/2020/08/03/vatican-ii-and-the-calvary-of-the-church.

the Work of the Spirit," bearing the subtitle: "His has been a severe grace, but also a beneficent grace."[46] For Weinandy—whose principled stance against the deviations of Pope Francis earned him both the enmity of officialdom and great respect from Catholics concerned with the current crisis[47]—Vatican II looks as though it precipitated a crisis because it exposed long-simmering and hidden evils. Doing so was a "necessary evil," like lacerating a boil or cauterizing a wound. For example, he writes: "It is naïve to think that so many priests, prior to the Council, were men of deep faith, and then, overnight, after the Council, were corrupted by the Council or the spirit of the Council, and so jettisoned their faith and left the priesthood." Fr. Weinandy also claims that Vatican II set into motion many good processes and initiatives that are bearing fruit today.

To Fr. Weinandy's point that the evils we see after the Council were present before the Council and were simply revealed by it, I would respond:

1. We have to distinguish among three groups in the Church before the Council. There were the corrupt, the confused, and the righteous. What was the effect of the Council on all three groups? Fr. Weinandy's point concerns mainly the corrupt: the Council brought them out into the open, where they indulged their errors and vices more freely. But he does not address the effect on the confused, which was to give them the impression that the way of the corrupt was legitimate, or at least no longer banned with a perpetual ban. Nor does he address the effect on the righteous, which was to reduce their ability to challenge the corrupt or influence the confused. Over a very long time, Fr. Weinandy's point may hold— namely, that it was a grace to expose all this evil; but that is entirely compatible with saying that bringing all this evil into the open also increased the evil. If the boil had to be lanced, it was lanced incom-

---

46. Letter #14 of *The Moynihan Letters* at *Inside the Vatican*, July 27, 2020, https://insidethevatican.com/news/newsflash/letter-14-2017-quest.

47. "Pope Francis and Schism," *The Catholic Thing*, October 8, 2019, www.the-catholicthing.org/2019/10/08/pope-francis-and-schism. Fr Weinandy has largely lost this respect by adding his name to a spectacularly ill-informed, risibly propangandistic, five-part series at *Church Life Journal* (September through November 2022) denigrating the traditional Mass and defending the Novus Ordo.

petently; the result was infection and amputation at the hands of the divine Surgeon.

2. One must not succumb to a subtle subjectivism. Suppose there were, all through the Church, corrupt priests thinking corrupt thoughts while they celebrated the Mass; suppose their celebration of the Mass was subjectively bad, although outwardly good. It is in fact a worse evil to have their Masses also *outwardly* bad. That is to say, adding the corruption of the visible ritual is in fact the addition of an evil. It would be like having lots of people who inwardly crave to be mass murderers (pun intended) and are then given free rein to act on their cravings: the net amount of evil does not remain the same just because intentions have not changed.

3. Defenders of the Council, who are usually also critics of the preconciliar era (especially the "1950s"), exhibit a strange optimism about human nature. The pessimistic realism of Catholic tradition would suggest that perhaps most Catholics most of the time adhere to some acceptable standard of morality and religious practice through a combination of habit, good custom, fear of being labeled a bad person, and fear of divine punishment. The virtues of the laity may rise to greater heights and certainly the preconciliar Church offered an abundance of ways and means for so advancing, but the Church in her maternal wisdom never held these less-than-stellar motives in contempt. The sheer magnitude and multitude of official changes during and after the Council turned the entirety of customary Catholicism inside-out in a campaign of unprecedented psychological cruelty and stupidity—assuming, for the sake of argument, that the intention of churchmen was to *retain* or even *increase* the faithful rather than to push them into restless experimentation, bewilderment of conscience, institutional disgust, or surrender to worldliness. No, it is simply not possible to buy the line that the chaos unleashed by the Council was a "necessary evil" or a "severe mercy." No Christian, not even a pope, is permitted to gamble with immortal souls. The idea that overthrowing the present order in the name of evangelical purity or fervor will somehow bring about a mature and positive Catholicism of the future is nothing but Marxist logic dressed up in church vestments. Such logic always requires feeding the Moloch of progress with copious sacrificial victims. In

any age of the Church, regardless of how "healthy" her people may be, a colossal upheaval will be accompanied by the falling-away of many, including clergy and religious. That the period from Vatican II onwards has been characterized by an exodus or drift into apostasy is not a sign of some kind of desperate fragility in the 1950s; it is a sign, rather, of the inherent fragility of fallen human nature, which relies on existing structures and a stable frame of meaning to a far greater extent than ivory-tower intellectuals seem to be aware.

To Fr. Weinandy's list of positive fruits of the Council, I would respond:

1. Some of his list is true, because God always brings good out of evil. Imploding religious orders made way for new and better ones, although the more traditional among them are now being persecuted by the Vatican II nostalgics.

2. Some of his list is true, because in fact the Council was not all bad. In the great scheme of things, I expect that John Paul II's pontificate will bear more theological fruit for the Church than the Council itself, but Fr. Weinandy is probably right that the Council was a condition of his election.

3. Some of his list is not quite true, because there were many good fruits germinating in the Church *before* the Council, and the Council echoed rather than squashed them. This is a key point: if Fr. Weinandy wants to say the evils already present but exposed after the Council cannot be attributed to the Council, then he will have to say the same for the goods that follow the Council. Not all good things that happened after the Council can be attributed to it; this would be a case of the same *post hoc ergo propter hoc* fallacy that antitraditionalists love to hurl at traditionalists. For example, the renewed use of Scripture in theology and the renewal of patristics were well underway before the Council and can be readily seen in the work of many theologians who, translated into today's ecclesiastical scene, would no doubt find themselves most at home among the traditionalists.

In short, Fr. Weinandy has overstated the case for keeping the Council relevant to the daily life of the Church.

I would not subscribe to the view that the Council should be "forgotten" as though it never happened. That is not how history works. Rather, it must be remembered—albeit with shame and repentance, as a moment in which the hierarchy of the Church, to varying degrees, surrendered to a more subtle (and therefore more insidious) form of worldliness. Moreover, the errors contained in the documents, as well as the many errors commonly attributed to the Council or prompted by it, must be drawn into a syllabus and anathematized by a future pope or council so that the controverted matters may be laid to rest, as former councils have wisely and charitably done in regard to the errors of their times.

Just as Viganò exposed the Vatican's and much of the hierarchy's complicity with evil in the case of Theodore McCarrick, so too he has turned a bright light on the doctrinal and liturgical evils that plague the Church because of the Council's orientations, decisions, and texts. It's no longer enough to point to some nifty things Vatican II said, or a few good things that have happened in the past half century. We know that already. It's also more than a bit silly at this point to say, "You know, the Church wasn't perfect before the Council," as if anyone ever asserted that it was.

Today, I find that most of those who attempt to "respond" to the Council's critics walk right past the important questions. It's as if they've arrived very late to a party where an in-depth conversation has been going on for a long time—in this case, ever since Archbishop Marcel Lefebvre's *They Have Uncrowned Him* and Dietrich von Hildebrand's *The Trojan Horse in the City of God*, among others—and the newcomers burst in with observations that were taken up and thrashed out hours before. After an awkward pause, the conversation resumes among the serious participants, while the interrupters stroll away for a cocktail, feeling satisfied that they've "made their point." Alas, it was beside the point; it didn't advance the discussion, but merely interrupted it.

What cannot be denied by any objective evaluation is that, between 1962 and 1965, there took place a "paradigm shift" with regard to the intimate interrelationship of identity, continuity, tradition, and culture. These were dissociated in a way that was radically uncatholic—and radically unstable.

16

Traditionalism: Fidelity, Resistance, Work of the Church[*]

JEAN-PIERRE MAUGENDRE

Paix Liturgique, Letter 889
October 11, 2022

EVERYTHING BEGAN WELL:

> The Council that has just opened is like a resplendent dawn that is
> rising over the Church, and already the first rays of the rising sun
> are filling our hearts with sweetness. Everything here breathes
> holiness and brings joy. We see stars shining in the majesty of this
> temple, and these stars, as the Apostle John testifies (Rev 1:20), are
> you!

So said good Pope John in his opening address to the Council on
October 11, 1962! The proposed program was biblically simple:

> The Church has never ceased to oppose errors. She has even often
> condemned them, and very severely. But today, the Bride of Christ
> prefers to use the remedy of mercy, rather than brandishing the
> weapons of severity; she responds better to the needs of our time
> by emphasizing the riches of her doctrine.

The method adopted was also perfectly clear:

---

[*] On Saturday, September 24, 2022, a symposium on the future of the traditional
Mass was held in Paris, bringing together nearly five hundred participants. The
great success of this event, co-organized in particular by the associations Oremus-
Paix Liturgique and Renaissance Catholique, was due to the quality of the interven-
tions and in particular that of Jean-Pierre Maugendre, President of Renaissance
Catholique: "Le traditionalisme: une fidélité, une résistance, une œuvre d'Église."
The translation was prepared by Peter Kwasniewski and published at *Rorate Caeli*
on October 12.

It is necessary for [the Church] to turn to the present times, which bring with them new situations, new forms of life and open up new paths for the Catholic apostolate. It is for this reason that the Church has not remained indifferent before the admirable inventions of human genius and the progress of science, which we enjoy today, and that she has not failed to appreciate them at their true value.

These intentions, which were undoubtedly very praiseworthy in substance, led in reality to what Jacques Maritain—who could not have been suspected of traditionalism, and even, if I may say so, was the "hidden imam" of the Vatican Council—called, in the *Peasant of the Garonne*, "kneeling before the world."

In a few years, a heritage of many centuries was thrown down; thousand-year-old habits were forgotten, cursed, castigated, and condemned. Mrs. Michu,[1] who had not read the Acts of the Council and had no intention of devoting ten seconds to it, observed with astonishment, in her parish:

• The abolition of the choir, that was all well and good but…

• The elimination of Latin; well, she didn't understand anything of it, but the objective was for *God* to understand—and *that* she understood.

• The appearance of a table in front of the altar—it was her neighbor who had provided it!

• The celebration of the Mass facing the people, which made the celebrant turn his back to the tabernacle, which seemed incongruous to Mrs. Michu, but not to the celebrant.

• The distribution of Communion in the hand; Mrs. Michu had seen children put the host in their pocket.

• The upheaval of the calendar and the suppression of the patron saint of the parish. She learned that even St. Philomena, the favorite saint of the Curé d'Ars, had disappeared in the turmoil.

• The destruction of confessionals.

• The banishment of kneeling.

1. A French idiom meaning the average homemaker.

• The suppression of Corpus Christi processions.

• The abandonment of the recitation of the Rosary.

And so on and so forth... Mrs. Michu did as another neighbor did; she decided not to go to church again, except for weddings and funerals. Her religion had been changed.

As Patrick Buisson reports in his important book *The End of a World*, quoting a good mother, wife of a mechanic: "Religion should not change, since what we are looking for is to be sure of something." For his part, Guillaume Cuchet notes, in the conclusion of his valuable work *How Our World Ceased to Be Christian*:

> This rupture within Catholic preaching created a profound discontinuity in the preached and lived contents of religion on both sides of the 1960s. It is so manifest that an outside observer could legitimately wonder whether, beyond the continuity of a name and the theoretical apparatus of dogmas, it is still the same religion.[2]

All this was imposed with an unheard-of brutality. This brutality was certainly in opposition to the official discourse on "listening, openness, dialogue, respect for others, and the acceptance of differences," but it was necessary because all these upheavals did not in any way respond to the demands of the Catholic faithful themselves.

A survey of August 13, 1976, in the heart of the "hot summer" (so called not only because of the heat wave of that year but also in reference to the traditional Mass celebrated by Archbishop Lefebvre in Lille, in front of thousands of faithful), published by the IFOP and the Progrès de Lyon, revealed the extent of the malaise. While 40% of regular churchgoers felt that the reforms initiated by Vatican II should be continued, 48% felt that the Church had gone too far in its reforms. To this figure, we must undoubtedly add the vast majority of those who had simply stopped practicing between 1965 and 1976. Even today, all the surveys conducted by the association "Paix Liturgique" confirm these opinions. Overall, *today* 30% of regular churchgoers would attend the traditional Mass if it were celebrated in their parish.

---

2. See also chapter 17.

While it is fashionable to denounce clericalism, the years follow-ing the Council were primarily those of unbridled clericalism in keeping with what Bishop Schneider analyzed in his indispensable work *Christus Vincit*: "The 'Vatican II' phenomenon appears to be an enormous spectacle of clerical triumphalism." The departure of Madame Michu from her parish did not upset her parish priest; certainly it was upsetting for the collection basket, but he had well assimilated the postulate "a thousand times repeated, that the evan-gelization of those who were far away could be done only after the eviction of all those who were only falsely close," according to Patrick Buisson's luminous synopsis. As a bishop quoted in Jean Madiran's review *Itinéraires* wrote: "The Church is moving from a sociological Christianity to an authentic Christianity."

Traditionalism is first of all *that*: a fidelity to beliefs, habits, behaviors on which the postconciliar years claimed to sound the death-knell. For centuries, the life of the French countryside had been punctuated by the Church: think of *The Angelus* by Millet, the processions of the Rogations, public prayers to attract God's bless-ings to the earth. The world had changed. Let us quote Bishop Paul-Joseph Schmitt, then bishop of Metz: "The transformation of civili-zation through which we are living entails changes not only in our external behavior but in the very conception we have of creation as well as of the Salvation brought by Jesus Christ" (*L'hérésie du XXème siècle*, Jean Madiran, p. 130). This is manifested in the words of a 1969 episcopal report: "To the scandal or laughter of modern man, a part (actually more and more reduced) of our liturgy con-tinues to ask of God what the peasant asks of fertilizer: a cosmic Sal-vation which makes God the substitute for our insufficiencies" (quoted by Rémi Fontaine in *Présent* 7726, November 10, 2012). Is this not confusing and opposing the first cause and the secondary causes?

The Church was no longer the sole ark of Salvation, but only a means "for man to become fully human," "an expert in humanity," in the words of Paul VI. The "tragedy" was that this experience, this turn to man, did not seem to arouse the enthusiasm of the crowds and of political decision-makers.

Quite logically, this revolution against tradition aroused resistance. Some priests refused to celebrate the *Novus Ordo Missae*, arguing that the Bull *Quo Primum* of Saint Pius V and its perpetual permission were the basis for their theological doubts, in line with the *Brief Critical Study of the New Order of Mass* by Cardinals Ottaviani and Bacci. All over France, lay people gathered, supporting the priests who continued to celebrate Mass according to the *"usus antiquior."* Let us mention, in my native Brittany, Doctor Pacreau in Brest, Professor Lozachmeur in Rennes. Salons, auditoriums, sports halls, the Wagram hall in Paris, welcomed a growing number of disoriented, bruised, wounded faithful, eager to remain faithful to the liturgy that had sanctified their fathers. Some priests remained faithful to the Mass of their ordination or returned to it after a few years of reformed practice. Let us mention Monsignor Ducaud-Bourget, Father Reynaud, Father Calmel (O.P.), Father Marziac, Father Réveilhac, Father Montgomery, Father Sulmont, Canon Porta, Canon Roussel, et al.

An intellectual resistance arose: let us mention the articles of Father Bruckberger (O.P.) in *L'Aurore*, those of Louis Salleron in *Carrefour* and his book *La Nouvelle Messe*. Overlooking the whole, the review *Itinéraires*, founded in 1956, recalls, in the sparkling and precise style of Jean Madiran, the reasons for this resistance:

> Christian children are no longer educated but degraded by the methods, practices, and ideologies that now prevail most often in ecclesiastical society. The innovations which are imposed in this society, rightly or wrongly claiming to be based on the last Council, and which consist in delaying and diminishing the instruction of revealed truths, and in advancing and increasing the revelation of sexuality and its spells, are creating a generation of apostates and savages throughout the world, each day better prepared to kill each other blindly. ("Fundamental Declaration of the Magazine *Itinéraires*")

These lines have not aged a bit. They underlie a reclaiming that is still relevant today, as it was written in the book of the same name:

> It is clear that the Christian people as a whole and the Catholic clergy can hardly spontaneously have the courage or the discernment to keep Sacred Scripture, the Roman Catechism, and the Catholic Mass; they cannot have the courage or the discernment

to keep them at all costs at the center of the education of children. For them to have this discernment and courage, they must be positively and sufficiently encouraged by the spiritual authority that God has established for this purpose. That is why, turning to the leaders of the ecclesiastical hierarchy, we make an uninterrupted complaint: Give us back the Scriptures, the Catechism, and the Mass! We are on our knees before the Successors of the Apostles, kneeling as free men (as Péguy said), begging them and calling on them for the salvation of their souls and for the salvation of their people. Let them give back to the Christian people the Word of God, the Roman Catechism, and the Catholic Mass. Until they do so, they are as good as dead. We ask them for our daily bread and they keep throwing stones at us. But these very stones cry out against them to heaven: Give us back the Holy Scriptures, the Roman Catechism, and the Catholic Mass! When the men of the Church do not want to hear it, we cry out our reclamation to earth and heaven, to the angels and to God!

While this appeal, first made in 1972, was not fully acted upon, it is undeniable that little by little what must be called the ban on the celebration of the traditional Mass was lifted—until the publication of the ill-fated motu proprio *Traditionis Custodes* on July 16, 2021.

However, traditionalist resistance quickly crystallized around a prestigious prelate, Archbishop Marcel Lefebvre, former Archbishop of Dakar, Apostolic Delegate for French Africa, Superior General of the Holy Ghost Fathers, founder in 1970 of the Priestly Fraternity of St. Pius X, and of the International Seminary of Écône. At a time when no priest was being trained to celebrate the traditional Mass, except in the seminary of Bishop de Castro Mayer in Campos, Brazil, Archbishop Lefebvre carried the hopes and expectations of the traditional world. He was thus, for years, the only bishop to train and ordain priests for the traditional Mass, which quickly got him in trouble with the Roman authorities, from the declaration of November 21, 1974, to the consecrations without a pontifical mandate of 1988, passing through the suspension *a divinis* of 1976.

This declaration of 1974 is one of the founding acts of the traditionalist resistance:

We adhere with all our heart and soul to Catholic Rome, guardian of the Catholic faith and of the traditions necessary for the maintenance of this faith, to eternal Rome, teacher of wisdom and truth. On the other hand, we refuse and have always refused to follow the Rome of neo-modernist and neo-Protestant tendencies, which was clearly manifested in the Second Vatican Council and after the Council in all the reforms that followed. All these reforms, in fact, have contributed and still contribute to the demolition of the Church, to the ruin of the priesthood, to the annihilation of the sacrifice and the sacraments, to the disappearance of religious life, to a naturalist and Teilhardian teaching in universities, seminaries, catechesis, teachings stemming from liberalism and Protestantism, condemned many times by the solemn magisterium of the Church. No authority, not even the highest in the hierarchy, can compel us to abandon or diminish our Catholic faith, clearly expressed and professed by the Church's magisterium for nineteen centuries.

Archbishop Lefebvre was not a party man: he responded to requests for priests made to him by the laity; he supported religious communities whose founders or foundresses refused, in conscience, the new liturgy, the new catechism, and the "refoundation" of the constitutions of their community in the conciliar sense desired by the decree *Perfectae Caritatis*. Let us mention here Dom Gérard Calvet, founder of the Benedictine abbey of Le Barroux; Father Eugène de Villeurbanne, founder of the Capuchins of Strict Observance, whose mother house is today in Morgon; Mother Hélène Jamet, who with the help of Father Calmel maintained the traditions of the Dominican Sisters of the Holy Name of Jesus in Brignoles; Mother Anne-Marie Simoulin, who came from the same congregation and settled in Fanjeaux; Mother Elisabeth de La Londe, foundress of the abbey of Benedictine nuns in Le Barroux; Mother Gertrude de Maissin, founder of the Benedictine abbey located today in Perdechat, and so forth.

In this context, an apostolic movement emerged, the MJCF (Mouvement de la Jeunesse Catholique de France), a true nursery of leaders and a school for the executives of the Tradition from which were born multiple Christian homes, a bishop, several abbots or superiors of religious communities (Le Barroux, Lagrasse, Morgon, the Missionaries of Divine Mercy), several Mother Abbesses or superiors of female religious communities (Le Barroux, Perdechat…). New religious communities emerged: the Fraternity of the Transfiguration in Mérigny, under the aegis of Father Bernard Lecareux; two Dominican communities: the Fraternity of Saint Dominic in Avrillé, near Angers, originally made up of members of the MJCF, and the Fraternity of Saint Vincent Ferrier in Chémeré-le-Roi, in the Mayenne region, with Father de Blignières and Father Guérard des Lauriers (O.P.).

From 1983, on the initiative of the Henri and André Charlier Center, a pilgrimage drew ever larger crowds at Pentecost from Notre-Dame de Paris to Notre-Dame de Chartres, in the footsteps of Charles Péguy. The message around which all are united could be summarized as follows: "Let us practice the religion of our fathers. Let us make the experiment of Tradition. Moreover, wherever it is allowed to flourish, this experiment proves conclusive."

Guillaume Cuchet, who is not to be suspected of traditionalism since he is a member of the editorial board of the Jesuit review *Etudes*, honestly observes:

> This departure from the culture of duty and obligation—a path on which the Church has preceded, in many respects, the civil world, especially the school and educational world—is a fundamental event it would be appropriate to ponder. In families and environments where this culture has been both maintained and modernized, transmission rates [of the Faith] have often been better.

Today, traditional communities represent 12–15% of priestly ordinations in France, well beyond the numerical weight of "trads" in the Catholic demographics in France. The traditional world as a whole is young and missionary. Young because of the large families that are formed there—"these Catholic families with their blond children," nicely mocked by Fabrice Luchini in the film *Alceste à bicyclette*. Young, because conversions are numerous, attracted by the triptych: "Transcendence, excellence, coherence."

Why does the ecclesiastical hierarchy persist in such a blatant denial of reality in the face of such facts? A mystery! A mystery that we can, however, try to illuminate by means of two particularly penetrating analyses. As Paul Vigneron wrote in *Histoire des crises du clergé français contemporain*, as early as 1976:

> It is not a question of being content to say, like an emperor appalled by four years of atrocious war: "We did not want this!" We must have the courage to ask ourselves the inevitable question: Here are thirty years during which we have been making "experiments," apostolic or otherwise; in which we have gone, without ever managing to find them, in search of new methods of prayer and discipline. After so many attempts, will we dare, at last, to risk one last one? Simply and loyally to try those methods of apostolate and spirituality that we had rejected, perhaps with temerity, some thirty years before? And if, by chance, these methods, which have proved their worth, were to succeed—who knows!—in giving us back the joy of heart that we have lost, if they filled our seminaries again, which have become almost deserted, if they gave back to our preaching and to our life that strength that only consecrated witnesses possess—would we dare to admit at last that we were mistaken?
>
> But here, precisely, is the hardest word to pronounce! After Christ's arrest, some of the apostles denied Him because they feared for their own lives. Today, it is much more than their lives that are at risk for those who have adhered—sometimes enthusiastically and without necessarily seeing the pernicious character thereof—to the innovative tendencies that appeared around 1945. They have now reached the age of influence and, sometimes, of high responsibility. It is their self-esteem that should be sacrificed by saying humbly: "Yes, perhaps we have been wrong for a long time!" Courageous men can, like the first apostles after their falling-away, finally sacrifice their lives to God... but can self-love?

Pierre Chaunu, the famous Protestant historian, wrote, for his part, in the conclusion of his work, published in 1975, *De l'histoire à la prospective*:

> Before the quantitative drying up of recruitment, it is an intellectual and spiritual drying up of vocations that has affected the Church in France since roughly 1930. The intellectual and spiritual mediocrity of the leaders in place in the Western churches at the beginning of the 1970s is distressing. An important part of the clergy of France constitutes today a social, intellectual, moral, and spiritual sub-proletariat; of the great tradition of the Church this

fraction has often kept only its clericalism, intolerance, and fanaticism. These men reject a heritage that crushes them, because they are intellectually incapable of understanding it and spiritually incapable of living it.

This reference to the ecclesiastical hierarchy is one of the major characteristics of the traditionalist movement. The consecrations of 1988 divided this world into two components united by the same faith, the practice of the same sacraments, the same will not to break from the hierarchical structure of divine right of the Church, the same concern for the social Kingship of Our Lord Jesus Christ.

A traditionalist "ecosystem" has been built, with its places of worship, its publications, its gatherings, its schools, its pilgrimages, etc. The risk would then be to sink into a communitarianism turned in on itself, oblivious to the challenges of the universal Church. To make Tradition a dead star, similar to what Russian Orthodoxy has become, of which Father Martin Jugie wrote in his work on Joseph de Maistre and the Greek-Russian Church: "For many centuries, the East has become accustomed to considering revealed doctrine as a treasure to be guarded, not as a treasure to be exploited; as a collection of immutable formulas, not as a living and infinitely rich truth that the spirit of the believer seeks to understand and assimilate ever better." Joseph de Maistre, in his work *On the Pope*, observed: "All these churches separated from the Holy See, at the time of the twelfth century, can be compared to frozen corpses whose forms the cold has preserved."

A fertile warning for those who might forget that the fight for Tradition is first and foremost a work *of the Church*. If the Church does not begin with Vatican II, neither does it take refuge, from Vatican II onwards, in structures that would be foreign to the visible and God-willed organization of the Church: the pope and the bishops. It is a great mystery, with sometimes terrible dilemmas! It is a call to allow ourselves to be guided by St. Gregory of Nyssa: "The right way is the way of the mountains." Let us recall that, according to Emile Poulat, "Church history is not a Corpus Christi altar of repose." If churchmen today appear occupied by a worldliness that is foreign to the Church, there is nevertheless only one Church whose seat is in Rome and whose head is the pope. The major drama of our time is that the same Church distributes to us, through the same channel and often at the same time, not only the means and the words of Salvation but also insipid and insignificant words, sentimental and philanthropic, without vigor for good nor vigor against the evil. Disfigured, sometimes too human or worldly, neither frankly Catholic and anti-modernist nor frankly modernist and anti-Catholic, the Church remains the Church, the only ark of Salvation.

The difficulties of the present time should not be a reason for discouragement, quite the contrary. If our elders might once have feared that the thread of our liturgical and doctrinal tradition would be broken altogether, our situation is no longer that one. We know that the future belongs to us because, through Tradition, we are linked to the Apostles themselves and thus to Christ. Fashions come and go. The Cross of Christ continues to protect us and enlighten us with its outstretched arms.

Finally, in this struggle, for it is a struggle—indeed, all of Christian life is a struggle—we will keep in mind the precious advice of Father Calmel, intrepid defender of the traditional Mass:

> Let us be witnesses to the faith, as were our brothers, the martyrs of the first centuries in the midst of violent persecution. They showed themselves to be not only strong and courageous, but also gentle and patient, and this because their souls were ardent with charity.

17

Anatomist of the Catholic Collapse in France and Beyond

JOHN PEPINO

Catholic World Report
September 13, 2022

CATHOLIC PRACTICE COLLAPSED IN THE WEST IN THE 1960s: the statistics are overwhelming.

France, the eldest daughter of the Church, went from 25% Sunday Mass attendance in the 1950s to less than 2% now; the collapse includes regions where *weekly* Sunday Mass attendance had reached 97% in the late 1950s (this applies also to Belgium, Québec, etc.). The qualitative argument "but they're better Catholics now!"—a subjective assessment amounting to soul-reading that never did, on the whole, convince—is seldom heard anymore.

This is a catastrophe which, for having occasioned an abundant but too seldom rigorous literature, remains unsatisfactorily addressed or explained. One used to hear that it would be for twenty-first-century historians to sort out the extent, causes, and effects of the mid-to-late-twentieth-century collapse of Western Catholicism.

They have begun to do so, and none more carefully, soberly, and instructively than French historian Guillaume Cuchet (b. 1973), professor of history at the University of Paris I-Panthéon-Sorbonne. The title of his principal work on the subject is blunt: *How Our World Stopped Being Christian: Anatomy of a Collapse.*[1] It is heavy on facts and figures (including statistical maps) and shuns frivolous speculation; for this reason, it has received a couple of prestigious

---

1. Guillaume Cuchet, *Comment notre monde a cessé d'être chrétien. Anatomie d'un effondrement* (Paris: Éditions Points, 2020).

book awards from the French State.[2] This book, and indeed the rest of Cuchet's production, contributes to our understanding of what happened while proceeding carefully and avoiding polemics.

As it does not yet exist in English, we here present its salient discoveries and analyses.

The first fact that Cuchet brings out—relying on the excellent preconciliar sociological work of Canon Fernand Boulard and others[3]—is the surprising vigor of French Catholicism from the 1930s to the early 1960s, when it could be said that in France, Catholics made up the "ultramajority" (p. 56): from a survey conducted in 1872 to Boulard's investigations in the early 1960s, 98% of French responders declared themselves to be "Roman Catholic." True, some areas were void of actual Sunday Mass attendance (the very regions whose clergy had rallied to the French Revolution in the 1790s, which were the same regions, it turns out, that had been sluggish in implementing . . . Trent!) while in others, all but the canonically impeded were at Mass every Sunday of the year (the Vendée, Flanders...). 94% of French children were baptized Catholic within three months of birth (as opposed to 30% within seven years today). Boulard's work, summarized in a famous map of Catholic practice, was on the whole reassuring to an episcopate that had been worried by a 1943 book asking whether France might not be mission territory (it is still invoked to claim that all was not well in the 1940s and '50s).[4] Indeed, during those decades, fully three quarters of missionaries overseas were French priests and religious of both sexes.

Next, Cuchet explodes a couple of myths regarding the timing of the collapse. Conventional Catholic historiography dated the "before and after" event to 1968. Conservatives saw in that year a generalized breakdown in traditional society (the famous "May

---

2. From the *Académie des Inscriptions et Belles Lettres* and from the *Centre national du livre.*

3. Fernand Boulard and Gabriel LeBras, *Carte religieuse de la France rurale* (Paris: Cahiers du Clergé rural, 1952); id. et al., *Matériaux pour l'histoire religieuse du peuple français, XIXe-XXe siècles,* 4 vols. (Paris: Éditions de l'École des Hautes Études en Sciences Sociales, 1982–2011).

4. H. Godin and Y. Daniel, *La France, pays de mission?* (Paris: Cerf, 1943).

1968" strikes among workers and students) that affected the patriar-
chal structure of the family, respect for authority generally, and religion specifically. Progressive Catholics blamed the slowing down or
even reversal of necessary Vatican II reforms; from this point of
view, Paul VI's 1968 encyclical *Humanae Vitae* affirming the immorality of contraception betrayed the Council, dashed the hopes of
ordinary Catholics, and helped empty the churches.

Cuchet, once again relying on the late-1960s work of Canon Boulard and others, shows that the collapse of practice among Catholics
in France dates to three years *before* 1968, very precisely to the year
1965. He calls it "the year of the drop-off (*décrochage*)" or "of the
collapse (*effondrement*)." As Cuchet points out, this reality puzzled
Boulard and the bishops he reported to at a time of "ideological
sanctuarization of the Second Vatican Council,"[5] although by then
the bishops, who could (unconsciously?) sense that certain hopes
had been misplaced, were no longer interested in such quantitative
studies. In fact, Boulard continued his research at the university and
carried on until his death in 1977. Cuchet had access to some of his
correspondence and interlocutors from the period 1965–1977; after a
time, it did dawn on Boulard that something drastic had happened.

Cuchet shows that 1965 is not only the year of the collapse in
terms of Mass attendance but also—and sometimes even more dramatically—in terms of confession (now "reconciliation"), baptism,
and extreme unction (now "anointing of the sick"). The figures he
marshals are starkly irrefutable.

The question Cuchet, a professional historian, had to broach was
that of causes. His reluctance to tread onto the minefield is palpa-
ble. Although the trend over several centuries had been a slow
decline of Catholicism, with a few dips (French Revolution) and
peaks (in the nineteenth century—think of the Curé of Ars and
Saint Thérèse—and after each of the World Wars), the collapse of
1965 is as steep and sudden as it was completely unexpected by anyone at the time, Boulard being the first among those startled at so

---

5. Cuchet, *Comment*, 98. *Sanctuarisation* is a French neologism on Cuchet's
part indicating that Vatican II as an event is a sort of Holy of Holies for the generation that lived it.

uncharacteristic an inflexion in the graphs he had been drawing for a generation. Why did it happen at *this* time?

Cuchet cautiously ventures the following (p. 144): "Where can this rupture, since rupture there was, possibly have come from? There must have been an *event* behind a phenomenon of this magnitude, at least to *provoke* it. My hypothesis is that it was the Second Vatican Council."[6] He does hedge by claiming that *a priori* the texts of the Council had little to do with the collapse, while granting that, perhaps, certain aspects of the liturgical reform or of the text on religious liberty might have contributed. But certainly, he adds, the text on liturgical reform did not minimize the importance of Sunday liturgy—quite the contrary!

Here are the causes he invokes, in outline:

1. The teaching of the council on religious liberty in *Dignitatis Humanae* (December 1965). The application of religious liberty could hardly concern society at large, since such a liberty had existed in the West for nearly two centuries. It was therefore applied *ad intra* as freedom of conscience to the manner in which Catholics approached their own religious obligations (pp. 146–47). This amounted to a permission for Catholics to make up their own minds regarding doctrine and discipline (today we would speak of "cafeteria Catholicism").

2. The discrepancy between "official Catholicism" after Vatican II and traditional popular piety. As an illustration of this factor, Cuchet notes that in shrines where this piety was respected, the collapse was far slower than in those in which new pastoral orientations were enforced (p. 148).[7]

3. In this connection, Cuchet (p. 149) points out that some elements of the liturgy, while seeming secondary to intellectuals, are actually psychological and anthropological determinants. He mentions the abandonment of Latin, changing pronouns to address

6. "D'où cette rupture, puisque rupture il y a eu, a-t-elle donc bien pu venir? Il faut qu'il y ait eu un *événement* derrière un phénomène de cet ordre, au moins pour le *provoquer*. Mon hypothèse est qu'il s'agit du concile Vatican II."

7. Quoting Fernand Boulard, "La Religion populaire dans le débat de la pastorale contemporaine," in B. Plongeron, ed., *La Religion populaire. Approches historiques* (Paris: Beauchesne, 1976), 27–49.

God ("Thou" vs. "you" in the English context), Communion in the hand, the minimization or scuttling of former obligations (see below), and so forth.

4. An often forgotten principle of the new pastoral orientations is their high standard of expectation regarding the level of commitment of Catholics, starting already in 1960 and generalized by 1965. Access to baptism for one's children required not only the promise to have one's child catechized (which was already the case), but also now a "preparation" of several months for the parents to undergo. If the pastor deemed the parents insufficiently committed, he might postpone the baptism—a reversal of the preconciliar urgency to baptize children as soon as possible. Matrimony in Church went from a sociological convention to a personal investment and a public declaration of faith from which many, for diverse reasons, shrank (sense of propriety, discretion, simple shyness...).

5. As concerns doctrine and changes in catechesis, Cuchet invokes a principle that nineteenth-century philosopher Théodore Jouffroy articulated: changes in official teaching turn humble folk into skeptics. Indeed, an institution that admits to having been wrong yesterday may well be wrong today, too.[8] In this respect, Cuchet focuses on the sudden silence in the pulpits (as tracked in parish bulletins giving the topic of the homily) regarding the four last things (Death, Judgment, Heaven, Hell);[9] it gave the impression that the clergy had either ceased to believe in them or no longer knew how to discuss them, even though these had been frequent sermon topics right up until the Council; historian Jean Delumeau spoke of a preconciliar "pastoral strategy of fear."[10]

6. More fundamentally, Cuchet speaks of "a collective exit from the culture of obligatory practice under pain of mortal sin." This practice was articulated in the list of obligations generally taught as

---

8. *Comment*, 149, referring to T. Jouffroy, "Sur le scepticisme de notre époque," in id., *Cours du droit naturel, professé à la Faculté des lettres de Paris* (Paris: Prévost-Crocius, 1834), 1–7.

9. The author here thanks Éamonn Gaines for correcting a mistake in the original version of this article.

10. J. Delumeau, *Sin and Fear: The Emergence of a Western Guilt Culture* (New York: MacMillan, 1990).

"Commandments of the Church": holy days "of obligation"; Sunday Mass; confession of sins; Easter Communion; fasting (Ember Days, Vigils, Lent); abstinence (all Fridays and some other days). While these obligations were at most softened (days of abstinence and fasting) but never suspended in the official texts, they were seldom mentioned any more. The gradual shrinking of the Eucharistic fast (traditionally no food or drink of any kind from midnight to Communion), begun by Pius XII in 1953 (water no longer broke it), led to its virtual extinction by Paul VI (the "one hour before Communion" Eucharistic fast) (p. 153). These modifications entailed social changes as well: anecdotally, Boulard noted the adverse effect that the end of Friday abstinence had on the fish markets of France. The permission to anticipate Sunday by attending Mass on Saturday evenings participated in the desacralization of Sundays, whose focus now shifted to leisure (which the now widespread ownership of television sets and automobiles made that much more available). As an aside, Cuchet mentions that at the time, the clergy viewed these effects in a positive light: a pastor could now be sure that those Catholics who still went to Sunday Mass or did penance on Fridays did so "more freely and more consciously" (p. 155).

7. Lastly, a decision was made that let out of the churches their most teachable demographic: children. Under the former catechetical system, 80% of French children attended Mass every Sunday (with or without their parents) in preparation for their "Solemn First Communion," a rite of passage complete with a fancy lunch at the restaurant and gifts from relatives. Whole classes, arrayed in little wedding dresses and dark suits (festooned with white fringed satin arm band and mother-of-pearl crucifix boutonniere), went through it at the age of twelve. Weekly attendance at Mass and monthly confession were required to be admitted to this socially resonant rite, after which young people tended to replicate their parents' attendance rates. By 1965, however, this system was judged to be "merely social" and hypocritical and was withdrawn along with its incentives, significantly raising the median age of the average congregation. Retired priests of the conciliar generation have confided to Cuchet that they felt liberated from such a burden as hearing confessions, particularly children's confessions, every Sat-

urday—a burden termed "chronophagous," a "time-eater." Other factors may have played a role in the loss of the church-attending hordes of children too, including the length of obligatory schooling, which gave the public school system a longer time in which to intervene between family tradition and the child.

Such, in broad strokes, are the results of Cuchet's careful analysis of and reflection on the data surrounding the unprecedented downturn in the graph tracking measurable religious practice among Catholics in France. There is no denying that, despite the author's charitable tone, it does amount to an indictment of the clergy (bishops and priests alike) on whom the responsibility of implementing the Council fell. Retrospectively, one wishes the priests had left well enough alone.

What emerges most forcefully—and what the author goes on to explore in his more reflective and prospective book *Does Catholicism Still Have a Future in France?*[11]—is the necessarily *sociological* dimension of religion. A whole complex of shared values, to some extent held together by a system of obligations indexed on a strong sense of the connection between religious practice and one's eternal destiny, and incarnated in seasonal practices (recurring feasts and fasts, rites of passage), was the *body* of Catholicism, while the *soul* in this analogy was actual personal assent to the truths taught and, *in fine*, commitment to Christ. Many of what Cuchet calls the clergy's "false good pastoral ideas" (i.e., good intentions with disastrous results) derive from the Platonic notion that separating the soul from the body would be to the former's benefit. Instead, of course, death ensued, and our world stopped being Christian.

It is most interesting to compare similar works in other countries—not least our own—to see whether the local situation, with its own particularities (the Church in the US did not have Solemn First Communion, nor was it ever the ultramajority), reflects the same statistical drop-off, and at what date (was it also 1965?); as it is, Cuchet's work may be too narrowly focused on France alone. But this work, in tandem with the statistical analyses of Stephen Bulli-

11. Guillaume Cuchet, *Le Catholicisme a-t-il encore de l'avenir en France?* (Paris: Seuil, 2021).

vant's *Mass Exodus: Catholic Disaffiliation in Britain and America since Vatican II* (Oxford, 2019) and, for religious life, Fr. Joseph Becker's significant *The Re-Formed Jesuits: A History of Changes in Jesuit Formation During the Decade* 1965–1975 (Ignatius, 1992),[12] may help to pinpoint and, perhaps, avoid repeating the causes of the major civilizational change of our lifetime.

12. Not to forget, on the order of anthropological principles, Mary Douglas's classic *Purity and Danger* (London: Routledge & Kegan Paul, 1966) and *Natural Symbols* (London: Barrie and Rockliff, 1970). Peter Kwasniewski kindly brought Douglas's work to my attention.

Vatican II at Sixty:
Time to Stop the Cheerleading

FR. JOHN PERRICONE

Crisis Magazine
October 11, 2022

ON OCTOBER 4, BASIC BOOKS RELEASED GEORGE WEIgel's latest work, *To Sanctify the World: The Vital Legacy of Vatican II*.[1] It left much of the Catholic world slightly confused, except for that dwindling minority still starstruck by Vatican II's promise of a "new Pentecost."

Far be it for any faithful Catholic to call into question its legitimacy or validity. With that full disclosure out of the way, isn't it possible—after sixty years—to ask some quite relevant questions about its expediency or its design? It seems Mr. Weigel is of a generation that accepted uncritically the *Weltanschauung* of a mid-twentieth century European Catholic elite still swooning over Roncalli's mirage of *aggiornamento*.

Call to mind that it was entirely of a piece with that dizzying headiness of going to the moon, supercomputers, and the Age of Aquarius. A time of the intoxications of Teilhard de Chardin and his beloved Noosphere, Rahner and his Anonymous Christian, and Hans Urs von Balthasar's *apokatastasis*. And even more: Sr. Corita Kent's "damn everything but the circus," Harvey Cox's *Secular City*, Rogerian Self-actualized Man—and who can forget the new frontiers of John Robinson's *Honest to God*. Ah, they were times that left men dreaming dreams. And every one of them became a nightmare.

Out of this fanciful period was Vatican II convened. Sadly, the

---

1. See chapters 21 and 22.

antinomian exuberance of the age fell like magical dust on more than a few of the Council's principal architects. When Pope John XXIII announced his intention to summon the Council, Cardinal Heenan of London warned, "This is tempting the Holy Ghost!" Why such a monition from an otherwise prim and circumspect British Prince of the Church?

Councils were only convened to confront great crises threatening the Church. Where was the crisis compelling this one? No Catholic could see one, but an elite of illuminati did.

It seems as though Mr. Weigel has been swept up in the dreamscape of those Catholic cognoscenti. After citing Pope John's opening address declaring that the "council's greatest concern" is presenting more fully "the sacred deposit of Christian doctrine," Mr. Weigel goes on to say, "That would not happen, however, if the Church merely guarded this (then quoting Roncalli again) 'precious treasure . . . as if we were only concerned with an antiquity.'"

Weigel proceeds to explain, "Nor would it suffice to repeat familiar formulas of faith, like those in the simple question-and-answer catechisms that Catholics had long known." For an otherwise sterling orthodox Catholic thinker, those are strange words indeed. How else can one explain them except to wonder that perhaps he inhaled too much of the questionable assumptions of the European *bien pensant*?

How else to comprehend this counterintuitive and utterly ahistorical defense of Roncalli's myopic vision?

> John XXIII knew that the defensive Catholicism of the Counter-Reformation, however successful a salvage operation, had run its course. It was time to raze the bastions that Catholicism had erected and turn its robust institutions into platforms for evangelization and mission in order to engage a deeply troubled modern world. The Church, he believed, existed to proclaim and compassionately witness the Christian truth for the world's healing and sanctification. It could not hide that truth like the frightened servant in Christ's parable of the talents.

Mr. Weigel seems to be parroting the Old Thinking of the septuagenarian and octogenarian Shepherds in the Church. This Old Guard is presently splenetic at the cry of young Catholics for the undiluted Ancient Faith rather than the Synodal Way that is so giddily embraced (and tightfistedly enforced) by their betters.

How could someone as gifted as Mr. Weigel repeat without embarrassment Roncalli's indictment of 500 years of Post-Reformation Catholicism as "guarding a precious treasure as though it were an antiquity"? He knows better than most St. Paul's mandate to Timothy: "*custodi depositum*" (guard the deposit). Yes, the Church jealously "guards" so that she can boldly proclaim. And, indeed, she did. And she did it with supernatural gusto during all those centuries to which Mr. Weigel happily bids a fond farewell.

Then there is this: "It was time to raze the bastions that Catholicism has erected and turn its robust institutions into platforms for evangelization and mission in order to engage a deeply troubled modern world." We expect this kind of cant from self-loathing Catholics, but not from a gifted Catholic intellectual of Mr. Weigel's rank. Was that summons due to a momentary memory lapse? Mr. Weigel pleads for a Church "to proclaim and compassionately witness to Christian truth for the world's healing and sanctification." Surely Mr. Weigel recalls the global and prodigious efforts of the Church in the past centuries doing just that. To name a paltry few:

• The Jesuits' monumental missionary efforts in South America, to say nothing of their staggering accomplishments in covering all of Europe with its finest educational institutions.

• St. Isaac Jogues' heroic efforts to bring the Holy Gospel to the Indians of North America.

• Fr. Junipero Serra's breathtaking missionary work and foundations in California.

• The Holy Ghost Fathers' dazzling missionary accomplishments in Africa.

• The Maryknoll Fathers' dauntless work in China, which accumulated for that Order countless numbers of martyrs.

• Innumerable religious orders of women who marched into Africa to open hospitals and schools.

• St. Katherine Drexel's founding of the Sisters of the Blessed Sacrament specifically to bring the Gospel to Native Indians and Blacks.

• The St. James Society, which sent scores of priests to work in the missions of South America.

• Mother Teresa's missionary work in India.

Was all of this evidence of a Church obsessed with "guarding antiquity"? Perchance Mr. Weigel was thinking of a Church insufficiently engaging the world on high intellectual matters? In that case, he certainly must know the amazing philosophical and theological work of Catholic scholars in those "fortress years" who transformed the intellectual landscape. To cite just some:

> • Jacques Maritain's guest professorships at Columbia, Princeton, and the University of Chicago, all the while publishing some of the most significant works on St. Thomas Aquinas and influencing the entire academic world.

> • Etienne Gilson's guest professorships at Harvard and the Sorbonne, as well as delivering the esteemed Gifford Lectures at the University of Aberdeen in Scotland.

> • Fr. Stanley Jaki's impressive oeuvre in reconciling physics and the sciences with the truths of the Faith.

> • Fr. Garrigou-Lagrange's work in Thomistic philosophy and his polemical works engaging the philosophies of the day.

> • Learned Catholic academic societies in every major scientific, literary, philosophical, and theological discipline.

Add to this impressive work of evangelization the fact of thousands of Catholic schools with an average student population of one thousand children; seminaries filled to capacity, and novitiates as well; religious brothers conducting some of the finest schools in America.

Does all of this sound like a Church enclosed in upon itself? This ever-mushrooming evidence of Catholic universal reach prompted the inimitable Karl Adam to write in his memorable 1934 *Spirit of Catholicism*:

> What [the Church] wishes to establish is the fact that human reason, while remaining true to itself, can by its own principles advance to a point where God becomes visible as the fundamental basis and ultimate meaning of all reality, and where knowledge passes over into faith, philosophy into theology. Whenever men

have doubted or denied the capacity of the human mind to transcend the limits of experience, whenever they have attempted to paralyze or kill man's profound yearning for absolute truth, then the Church has come forward in defense of reason, whether against Averroes and Luther or against Kant. And the more our own age becomes weary of subjective idealism and seeks to rediscover the objective world, the more grateful will it be to Pope Pius X that in his much abused anti-Modernist Encyclical *Pascendi* he denounced all positivism, pragmatism and phenomenalism and defended the power of reason to transcend and surpass experience, thus exorcising those twin bugbears of solipsism and skepticism which menace all knowledge.

If Vatican II deserves all the encomia showered upon it by the Old Thinking, then how does one explain the censorious comment of Pope Paul VI, in 1972, that "the smoke of Satan has entered the Church"? Lest I be accused of committing the *post hoc ergo propter hoc* fallacy, we must be clear that there is no cause-effect between Vatican II and Montini's lament. But their uncomfortable proximity raises eyebrows. To quote Mark Twain, "history does not repeat itself, but it rhymes." Clearly, the "smoke of Satan" was not a consequence of Vatican II, but it does seem to rhyme.

Moreover, the vigorous stretching that Pope Benedict XVI performed in articulating a "hermeneutic of continuity" is demonstration that Vatican II could not stand alone. It contained undeniable weaknesses. They could only be redressed by supplying the necessary unambiguous statements made by the Church's Magisterium. Other ecumenical councils never required such embarrassing backtracking. Their reasoning was as tight as a drum and the meaning of their words as clear as the sun.

Isn't it time to move past the Old Thinking that lauded Vatican II? With all due respect to the Second Vatican Council, it does not meet the demands of a secular world. For that we need a virile, unequivocal, and full-throated Catholicism.

Yes, take from Vatican II what was good, but stop the cheerleading. It is simply unseemly of an intelligent and faithful Catholic.

Mr. Weigel, isn't it time to admit that the bloom has come off the rose?

19

Vatican II at Sixty:
Time for Retirement

ERIC SAMMONS

Crisis Magazine
October 11, 2022

TODAY IS THE SIXTIETH ANNIVERSARY OF THE OPENING of the Second Vatican Council. Undeniably the most influential event in modern Church history, Vatican II impacted every facet of Church life, from how the pope exercises his ministry to how parishes operate.

Since Vatican II, however, the Church has suffered many losses: millions leave the flock every year, the Church's moral standing in the world is shattered, and she is deeply divided.[1] While a small (but vocal) segment of Catholics places the blame for these losses at the feet of the Council, most Catholic leaders, particularly among the ranks of the bishops, argue that we must look to Vatican II to reverse these disturbing trends: only through the Council can we revitalize the Church. Some argue that this will be done by correcting mis-implementations of the Council, while others fight for a "fuller" implementation, in line with the "spirit of Vatican II." But perhaps there is a better option, one that leaves behind the rancorous debates that have dominated Church life for decades: retiring the Council.

Of course, retiring Vatican II is anathema in most Church circles today, especially in chanceries and rectories. Not a week goes by without a bishop or priest or Catholic public figure arguing for the

---

1. See my article "The Multiple Religions Coexisting Within the Catholic Church," *Crisis Magazine*, September 29, 2022, www.crisismagazine.com/2022/the-multiple-religions-coexisting-within-the-catholic-church.

need to continue implementing the reforms of Vatican II. Pope Francis in particular sees the Council as the instrument through which the Church is reformed. His views are shared by many bishops, even those who differ with the pontiff on how such a reform would take place.

The desire among bishops and other Church leaders to either continue or restart the implementation of Vatican II may be well-intentioned in that it recognizes our crisis and our need for reform. Whether it is wanting a liturgy more faithful to *Sacrosanctum Concilium*, or a more expansive ecumenism in the light of *Unitatis Redintegratio*, or a better understanding of the role of the laity in keeping with *Lumen Gentium*—no matter if the desire for reform comes from a "conservative" or "liberal" perspective—all share a common presupposition: the problems of today's Church will be solved by looking to Vatican II.

After sixty years, though, is that presupposition still valid?

Pope Paul VI, soon after Vatican II ended, noted the Council's "pastoral character." After all, pastoral concerns—not doctrinal debates—dominated the agenda at the Council. While the doctrinal sections of the Council documents mostly re-stated traditional teachings, the emphasis—and purpose—of these texts was to give pastoral advice on how the Church should operate in the twentieth century. The Church, however, is quite different now.

This is the nature of pastoral advice: it is typically time-limited. How the Church ministers to the world has certain timeless principles, to be sure, but the details of how this ministry occurs change over time. The pastoral needs of Christians in the second century, for instance, are radically different from those in the twelfth century or in today's twenty-first century.

Yet doesn't the pastoral advice given by an ecumenical council of the Church transcend generations? Actually, no. The Council of Nicaea in the fourth century decreed that bishops should not be transferred to another diocese (a common practice today). The Fourth Lateran Council in the thirteenth century stated that Jews should not hold public office. The Council of Vienne in the fourteenth century ordered bishops to publicly condemn any priests who "engage in the butcher's trade." Pastoral advice, even from an ecumenical council, clearly can have limitations to specific times and places.

So the question no one seems to be asking is the one that should be addressed: is the pastoral advice given sixty years ago at Vatican II still applicable today? The world and the Church have changed immensely over those six decades, and many of the concerns of that time are not our concerns. The Council Fathers were not facing a Church which had lost millions of members to secularism and evangelicalism. They weren't part of a Church with almost no moral standing in the world. Their flock did not consist of the woefully under-catechized as it does today. The sexual revolution was only in its embryonic stages; now it's a demented adult.

The Council Fathers, in other words, were children of their times. They could not see into the future to know what challenges the Church would face in the twenty-first century. No matter how well-intentioned they may have been, they were still human beings with finite knowledge.

Of course, in the light of Church and world history, sixty years might not seem like that much time. It's likely, for instance, that the issues the Church faced in the year 760 were similar to those faced in the year 820. But due mostly to technological advances, the pastoral needs of the modern world shift much more rapidly. The past 100 years alone have seen more changes in how humans live than occurred in the 1,000 years prior.

Two examples should bring this point home. One of the often-ignored factors in the decline of Catholicism in the West is the rise of the suburbs. The life of the average Catholic parish in the West radically changed over the course of the twentieth century: from the hub of a geographically small local community to a Sunday pitstop in a car-dominated life. The growth of suburbs began before the Council, to be sure, but its impact was little understood or even acknowledged at that time. Using Vatican II as our pastoral model, however, results in either ignoring this issue altogether or forcing an awkward Vatican II solution onto a twenty-first century problem.

Another major factor in the decline of Catholicism—and religion in general—didn't even exist in the early 1960s: the internet. The ways in which the internet has changed how we live, how we conduct our relationships, and how we form communities are extreme. And while Vatican II did issue a decree on social communications, the Council Fathers had no way of anticipating the adverse consequences the internet and particularly social media would have on the practice of religion.

With rapid world changes comes the need for new pastoral advice, not advice bound to a different time's council. Just as we don't turn to the Third Lateran Council for pastoral advice today, so we shouldn't look to Vatican II anymore. The advice given by bishops in the early 1960s simply doesn't resonate today; it addresses a different time and a different Church culture. Looking slavishly to Vatican II as the primary means for guiding the Church today only hamstrings efforts for authentic reform.

Thus I propose that we "retire" Vatican II. We leave behind the acrimonious debates about the Council and recognize that whether Vatican II was a good council, a good council with a bad implementation, or a bad council is an irrelevant question. We no longer debate the merits of VHS over Betamax. Trying to drag Vatican II into the twenty-first century isn't helping to save souls.

After sixty years of controversy and conflict, Vatican II has earned its retirement. The Council can no longer be a lens for reform; we must see the Church and her mission with new eyes. Let's give Vatican II a golden watch, retire the council, and restart the work of evangelizing the world.

20

Did Anyone Outside the Church
Really Care about Vatican II?

KARL GUSTEL WÄRNBERG

The Catholic Herald
October 17, 2022

LAST WEEK SAW THE CELEBRATION OF THE FEAST OF ST John XXIII as well as the anniversary of the opening of the Second Vatican Council, which he convened.

The (by all accounts) humorous Pope spoke of "opening the windows to the world" and speaking in a "modern vernacular."

While the sentiment espoused by the Pontiff is admirable, the legacy of the council remains a vexed question in the Church. Is it to blame for the decrease in Mass attendance and the dwindling number of vocations? Or was it a change of direction which led the Church to a much-needed closer interaction with the world?

At face value, the idea of speaking in the "modern vernacular" strikes me as rather self-evident. People can't communicate easily if they don't speak the same language, and language—for better or worse—changes. There is an entire academic field founded in Germany called *Begriffsgeschichte*, known in the English-speaking world as "Conceptual History," devoted to the changing nature of concepts.

Nevertheless, the idea that Vatican II spoke to modernity is a double lie. Firstly, Vatican II spoke to its age, which has long since passed. Today's youth are not the youth of the '60s whom the Church was attempting to reach.

Secondly, no council has been more "Thomist" than the Second Vatican Council. While it was the First Vatican Council that declared it an article of faith that God's existence can be known by reason alone, and it was Pope Leo XIII who later spoke of a need to study St Thomas, it was the generation of Council Fathers attending Vatican II who were steeped in the speculations of the Angelic Doctor. A belief that a return to St Thomas would somehow be the answer to all of the Church's problems is simply posturing.

There is, however, a larger problem. Once the Church had decided to speak the language of the times, the times had already decided that they wouldn't listen.

The Church has always been in dialogue with its times, hence the common saying, *Ecclesia semper reformanda est* ("the church is always reforming"). But the reform, in this context, is not to be equated with change.

As the great statesman and father of conservatism Edmund Burke suggested: one must change in order to preserve. Burke himself hailed from Catholic stock and knew of Catholic natural law teaching, even taking to the streets to defend Catholics in the Gordon Riots.

The Church reforms itself when it finds new ways of accurately explaining the mysteries of which it is the steward. Revelation ended with the death of St John the Apostle, but theologians are tasked with unfolding and explaining the full meaning of the mysteries. In this sense, there is no new revelation, but we come to a more intimate knowledge of the mysteries when we reflect on them. Yet, behind the theologizing, there is a philosophical framework that needs to be addressed, and the contemporary framework of the world is one that refuses the questions that theology can answer. That is a problem Vatican II seems to have ignored entirely.

The answer to the question of what the full legacy of Vatican II is remains too early to tell. Many are angered by the "spirit" of the Council which is blamed for bringing in guitars, extraordinarily ordinary extraordinary ministers distributing communion, and polyester chasubles. Others welcome change and hope the Church will not only change externally but somehow adapt its internal core to the message of the world.

The fact is that the Church cannot change, at least not fundamentally. If it were to change fundamentally, it would no longer be the Church—it would be merely one amongst many other Christian institutions. This is not what Burke would've meant by changing in order to preserve. What he meant was that a revolution presents a fundamental change, while evolution is a law of nature.

The question for many today is whether Vatican II was a revolution or an evolution. Perhaps the more pressing question, given the Council's aim, is: Did anyone outside of the Church really care?

21

What Vatican II Accomplished[*]

GEORGE WEIGEL

Wall Street Journal
September 30, 2022

THE SECOND VATICAN COUNCIL, WHICH OPENED SIXTY
years ago on October 11, 1962, was the most important Catholic
event in half a millennium. Its achievements were many and notable; it was also followed by ecclesiastical upheavals that continue to
roil the Church today.

After Vatican II, Catholics worshiped in their own languages,
rather than in Latin. By urging Catholics to become more biblically
literate, the council inspired lay communities of spiritual renewal,
some of them robustly charismatic. It also led to greater lay participation in all aspects of Church life: liturgical, educational, managerial, evangelical. The council fully inserted Catholicism into the
ecumenical movement's quest for Christian unity, even as it dramatically reconfigured the Church's relationship to its religious par-
ent, Judaism.

Vatican II was also the moment in which Catholicism fully realized its claim to be a global ("catholic") institution, as churchmen
from outside the Church's historic European core began to take
prominent roles in shaping the Catholic future. The extraordinary
growth of the Catholic Church in sub-Saharan Africa—where
Catholicism now counts hundreds of millions of adherents, many of
them first- or second-generation Christians—was accelerated by the
council's promotion of native African clergy and religious orders,

---

[*] This article was adapted from George Weigel's new book *To Sanctify the World:
The Vital Legacy of Vatican II* (New York: Basic Books, 2022).

its disentanglement of Catholicism from colonialism, and its insistence on the Church's essentially missionary character.

Had there been no Second Vatican Council, the Catholic Church of the twenty-first century would look rather different. So would world politics. The council's seminal Declaration on Religious Freedom, which recognized that the altar-and-throne alliances of the past were not possible under modern political conditions, helped to transform the Church from a bulwark of the status quo into one of the world's foremost institutional defenders of basic human rights. Absent Vatican II, it is difficult to think of a pope coming from Poland or to imagine that pope playing a pivotal role in one of contemporary history's great transformations: the self-liberation of Central and Eastern Europe in the 1989 collapse of European communism.

On this sixtieth anniversary, however, critics of Vatican II and its implementation will emphasize other realities of postconciliar Catholic life. In the decade after the council concluded on December 8, 1965, tens of thousands of priests and religious sisters abandoned their rectories and convents, in the largest such exodus since the sixteenth-century Reformations. The council wanted the Mass, the central act of Catholic worship, to be more accessible and participatory, thereby giving Catholics a deeper sense of the spiritual amplitude within which this world exists. Instead, the Mass was too often dumbed down into banality, if not downright silliness.

Catholic activists, especially in Latin America, tried to concoct an impossible synthesis between Christianity and Marxism, with disastrous political, economic, and social results still evident in places like Venezuela, Nicaragua, Peru, and even Mexico. The once-thriving Catholicism of Western Europe—countries whose theologians and bishops were the principal movers-and-shakers at Vatican II— has largely disappeared since the council, replaced by a Church of the Zeitgeist that seems far more liberal-Protestant and woke-progressive than Catholic. Postconciliar breakdowns in seminary training and the discipline of the clergy were major contributors to the crimes of clerical sexual abuse. And then there is the scandal of Catholic public officials who, inaccurately claiming the warrant of Vatican II's call for a dialogue with the world of political power, promote public policies that contradict both Catholic teachings and the moral truths the Church holds we can know by reason.

Given that mixed picture over the past six decades, the question inevitably poses itself on this diamond anniversary: Was Vatican II really necessary?

It was.

Understanding why means coming to grips with the full truth about Pope John XXIII and his purposes for the council he summoned. And that requires getting beyond the mythology of Pope John as a jolly old Italian *nonno* (grandfather) who wanted to let a thousand ecclesiastical flowers bloom.

Angelo Giuseppe Roncalli, elected Bishop of Rome on October 28, 1958, as an elderly placeholder, took a different path to the papacy than many of his predecessors. They were the sons of aristocrats or socially well-placed professionals; his people were dirt-poor northern Italian peasants. Rather than being a theologian or a canon lawyer, his intellectual interest was history, and especially the Church-reforming work of St. Charles Borromeo in sixteenth-century Milan—a previous moment of social, political, and ecclesiastical turmoil.

An Italian army chaplain in World War I, Roncalli was a Vatican diplomat in the Balkans, Greece, and Turkey during the cataclysm of World War II. In those largely non-Catholic European peripheries, he provided Jews fleeing the Nazi Holocaust with false baptismal certificates and helped facilitate Jewish emigration to Palestine. Immediately after the war, he was sent as Vatican representative to a shattered, demoralized France. There, he witnessed a local Church, bitterly divided between royalists and republicans since the French Revolution, struggle to reignite Christian faith among alienated workers and existentialist intellectuals.

Promoted to Patriarch of Venice and given the cardinal's red hat as the Catholic equivalent of the faithful employee's gold watch, Roncalli experienced the Italian Church's weaknesses beneath what seemed to be its rock-solid position in society and culture. All this gave him a distinctive optic on the mid-twentieth-century pathologies of world civilization and convinced this conservative man of traditional piety that the Church's approach had to change.

In 1962, the influential German magazine *Der Spiegel* editorialized admiringly that, after 2,000 years, the Catholic Church "had achieved a unity and consistency in teaching and structure never seen before.... It possesses 'a single truth' and a single custodian of that truth." The "custodian" knew better. From his historical studies and pastoral experience, John XXIII knew that the defensive Catholicism of the Counter-Reformation, however successful a salvage operation, had run its course. It was time to raze the bastions that Catholicism had erected and turn its robust institutions into platforms for evangelization and mission in order to engage a deeply troubled modern world. The Church, he believed, existed to proclaim and compassionately witness to Christian truth for the world's healing and sanctification. It could not hide that truth like the frightened servant in Christ's parable of the talents (Luke 19:12–28).

In Pope John's adult lifetime, that world had come close to committing civilizational suicide twice, in two global wars that took perhaps eighty million lives. The world was now precariously balanced on the razor's edge of an even greater catastrophe, nuclear war. Such a world, materially rich but spiritually impoverished, needed a positive, ennobling vision of human nature, human community, and human destiny. The dangers confronting humanity, John XXIII believed, were the byproducts of false ideas about who we are, how we ought to live together, and where the human story was going. By re-energizing the Church for a mission of proclaiming the truths about our humanity revealed in the person, teaching, and work of Jesus Christ, the incarnate Son of God, Vatican II would help the world rediscover humanity's true "dignity [and] purposes," as the pope put it in the document solemnly convoking the council.

In his opening address to Vatican II, John XXIII suggested how ecclesiastical renewal would take place. The council, he said, should rekindle the evangelical fire of Christocentric faith that had animated the first Christians and their bold mission. "Christ Jesus," the octogenarian pope boldly claimed, "still stands at the center of history and life." Reanimated by that conviction, the Church would develop the means to express ancient and enduring truths in ways that modernity could hear.

Contrary to the claims of those votaries of Pope Francis who claim that the council instituted a "paradigm shift" in the Church's self-understanding, John XXIII did not convoke Vatican II to reinvent Catholicism. As he put it in his opening address, the council's "greatest concern" must be the more effective presentation of Catholic truth in full, what the pope called "the sacred deposit of Christian doctrine."

That would not happen, however, if the Church merely guarded this "precious treasure . . . as if we were only concerned with an antiquity." Nor would it suffice to repeat familiar formulas of faith, like those in the simple, question-and-answer catechisms that Catholics had long known. The Church had to do more, and Pope John borrowed from the work of the great English theologian, John Henry Newman, to describe a truly Catholic development of doctrine: "What . . . is necessary today is that the whole of Christian doctrine . . . be more fully and profoundly known . . . [and] presented in the way demanded by our times. For the deposit of faith, the truths contained in our venerable doctrine, are one thing; the fashion in which they are expressed, but with the same meaning and the same judgment, is another thing."

So the Church would propose, and in a vocabulary that the people of the modern world could hear and engage. The council was not summoned, however, to discard the essential truths that the Church had proposed for two millennia. For as the pope went on to say, "it is clearer than ever before that the truth of the Lord remains forever" (Psalm 116:2). Moreover, that "truth of the Lord" is, in fact, the Lord himself: "To the human race, laboring under so many difficulties, [the Church] says, as Peter once did to the unfortunate man who begged him for alms, 'Silver and gold have I none, but what I have I give you: in the name of Jesus Christ the Nazarene, rise and walk'" (Acts 3:6). Jesus Christ, not the Church, must be the center of the Catholic proclamation.

The more radical Catholic traditionalists of our day seem to imagine that the Catholic bastion of the mid-twentieth century could have sustained itself indefinitely. If that were true, however, why did that way of being Catholic crumble so quickly in Ireland, Québec, Spain, and Portugal? And why did those men and women most recently formed in preconciliar seminaries and novitiates lead the flight from the priesthood and consecrated religious life?

Thoughtful assessments of Vatican II and its legacy must acknowledge that the preconciliar Catholic past was more brittle and fragile after two world wars, and more vulnerable to the cultural tsunami of the 1960s, than some nostalgic traditionalists imagine. Moreover, bunker Catholicism is a betrayal of the great commission that was central to John XXIII's original intention for Vatican II: "Go . . . and make disciples of all nations, baptizing them in the name of the Father and of the Son and of the Holy Spirit, teaching them all that I have commanded you" (Matthew 28:19–20).

Sixty years after Pope John opened the council by proposing a Christ-centered humanism capable of animating just and humane societies, an empirical fact is worth noting: Amid crises, challenges, and persecutions, the flourishing parts of the world Church today are those that have accepted his call to a mission that offers friendship with Jesus Christ as the answer to the question that is every human life, and that live that mission compassionately in the fullness of Catholic faith.

By contrast, those sectors of the world Church that have taken Vatican II as an invitation to teach and live Catholic Lite are demonstrating that Catholic Lite leads inevitably to Catholic Zero. In 2022, the vibrant parts of a globalized Catholicism are those living John XXIII's original intention for Vatican II as a council that would renew the Church for its mission of sanctifying an often claustrophobic, self-absorbed, and frightened world. Those that misconstrue Vatican II as a call to embrace secular modernity uncritically rather than to engage and convert it are dying, because they fail to offer the world a Christ-centered medicine for its ills.

John XXIII often spoke of his hope that Vatican II would be a "new Pentecost," recalling the descent of the Holy Spirit on the Apostles. The council he imagined was not a business meeting in which the branch officers of a global enterprise discussed ways to increase market share in a stable cultural and social environment. Pope John intended Vatican II to be an event in the realm of the spirit: an experience of the love of God breaking into the world anew. That experience, this man of deep faith hoped, would not only console but re-enliven a world beset by the fear that is the corrosive byproduct of spiritual emptiness.

Realizing that intention remains a noble and urgent task for Catholics today.

22

Why Vatican II Was Necessary[*]

GEORGE WEIGEL

First Things
October 19, 2022

WRITING MY NEW BOOK, *To Sanctify the World: The Vital Legacy of Vatican II* (Basic Books), afforded me the welcome opportunity to dig into the Council's sixteen texts and the many fine commentaries on them. It also made me ponder why the Council was necessary. That question is often raised today by young Catholics who, unsettled by the excessive ecclesiastical air turbulence over the past decade and generally ill-informed about the preconciliar Church, imagine that everything in Catholicism was copacetic until John XXIII made the fatal mistake of summoning an ecumenical council. That, however, was not the view of some quite orthodox Catholic leaders in the decade before Vatican II.

Msgr. Giuseppe De Luca was a stalwart churchman who had drafted the Holy Office decree placing the books of 1947 Nobel Prize-winner André Gide on the Index of Forbidden Books. In 1953, however, he found the atmosphere in the Holy Office, the *suprema* among curial offices, insufferable. So he vented his frustrations to Msgr. Giovanni Battista Montini (the future Pope Paul VI) in these no-nonsense terms: "In this suffocating atmosphere of unctuous and arrogant imbecility, perhaps a scream—chaotic but Christian— would do some good."

Then there was the Swiss polymath-theologian Hans Urs von Balthasar. In 1952, he published a small book in German, *Razing the Bastions: On the Church in This Age,* in which he worried that the

---

[*] This article was adapted from *To Sanctify the World: The Vital Legacy of Vatican II* (Basic Books, 2022).

great Catholic tradition had become fossilized and had "slipped out of the [Church's] living center of holiness." The "great salvage operation" of the Counter-Reformation had been necessary, Balthasar argued, but it was over, and the Church had to get out of its defensive crouch and get on with offering humanity the truth of God in Christ.

In the years immediately after the Council, Joseph Ratzinger (the future Pope Benedict XVI), who was one of the three most influential theologians at Vatican II, knew that the Council's reception was imperfect and its implementation even more imperfect. Nonetheless, he identified further reasons why Vatican II was necessary and why its teaching was essential for the Church's life going forward:

> [The] Council reinserted into the Church as a whole a doctrine of [papal] primacy that was dangerously isolated; it integrated into the one *mysterium* of the Body of Christ a too-isolated conception of the hierarchy; it restored to the ordered unity of faith an isolated Mariology; it gave the biblical word its full due; it made the liturgy once more accessible; and, in addition, it made a courageous step forward toward the unity of all Christians.

Thus the Council had many theological and doctrinal accomplishments to its credit. These were crucial to rekindling that radical, Christ-centered faith that would be the source of a revitalized Catholic mission to convert the modern world. Similarly, the Council's rejection of Catholic triumphalism was good in itself and necessary for its mission: "It was both necessary and good for the Council to put an end to the false forms of the Church's glorification of self on earth, and by suppressing her compulsive tendency to defend her past history, to eliminate her false justification of self."

That having been done, however, Ratzinger believed that continual, obsessive self-flagellation put another obstacle in the path of evangelization and mission. Unlocking the promise of the Second Vatican Council meant renewing our faith in the Lord's pledge "to be with you always" (Matt. 28:20). So, the future pope concluded, "it is time ... to reawaken our joy in the reality of an unbroken community of faith in Jesus Christ. We must rediscover that luminous trail that is the history of the saints and of the beautiful—a history in which the joy of the Gospel has been irrefutably expressed throughout the centuries."

That reference to "the saints and the beautiful" helps us understand another reason why Vatican II was necessary. The Church's preconciliar proclamation and apologetics were strong on logic. But a world become irreligious—not pagan, for paganism had a sense of this world's englobement in a greater reality, but *irreligious*, tone-deaf to rumors of angels—was not, in the main, going to be converted by logical demonstrations. It would be converted by holiness, manifest in the lives of those who had become friends of the Lord Jesus Christ and joined themselves to his cause. It would be converted by the Church offering more beauty than the world could manage to create.

Where Catholicism is alive today, and Vatican II well-received and implemented, it is because local churches have embraced holiness and beauty as evangelical and catechetical pathways toward a Christocentric future.

About the Authors

ABBÉ CLAUDE BARTHE entered the seminary of the Priestly Fraternity of Saint Pius X in Écône, where he was ordained in 1979 by Marcel Lefebvre. Having left the Society, after a period of "canonical limbo" he was incardinated in 2005 into the diocese of Fréjus-Toulon. He has taught for the seminary of the Institute of the Good Shepherd and the Institute of Christ the King Sovereign Priest and has published numerous liturgical studies. He also serves as chaplain of the annual Populus *Summorum Pontificum* Pilgrimage in Rome.

CHRISTIAN BROWNE is a practicing attorney in New York state. A board member of the Nassau County Catholic Lawyers Guild, he earned his J.D. from Fordham University in 2004. He published a historical play, *The Pearl of Great Price: Pius VI and the Sack of Rome* (Arouca, 2019).

MADOC CAIRNS is staff writer at *The Tablet* and a freelance writer with the *Observer*, the *Guardian*, and *Times Literary Supplement*, among others.

PHILLIP CAMPBELL holds a BA in European History from Ave Maria University and a certificate in Secondary Education from Madonna University. He is the author of the popular "Story of Civilization" series by TAN Books, as well as *Heroes and Heretics of the Reformation* and *Power from on High*. Campbell is also the founder of Cruachan Hill Press, which specializes in works of Catholic history and spirituality. He is the creator of the blog and website *Unam Sanctam Catholicam*.

LARRY CHAPP is a retired professor of theology. He taught for twenty years at DeSales University near Allentown, Pennsylvania. In

2013 he and his wife opened the Dorothy Day Catholic Worker Farm in Harveys Lake, Pennsylvania. Dr. Chapp received his doctorate from Fordham University in 1994 with a specialization in the theology of Hans Urs von Balthasar.

JOHN DANIEL DAVIDSON is a senior editor at *The Federalist*. His writing has appeared in the *Wall Street Journal*, the *Claremont Review of Books*, the *New York Post*, and elsewhere.

REV. RAYMOND DE SOUZA studied economics and political science before completing his seminary formation at St. Philip's Seminary in Toronto and at the Pontifical North American College in Rome (STB, Pontifical Gregorian University; STL, Pontifical University of the Holy Cross). He was ordained priest on July 20, 2002 for the Archdiocese of Kingston, Ontario and serves as pastor of Holy Cross Church in Kemptville, Ontario. Fr de Souza teaches at Queen's in the Department of Economics and writes regular columns for a number of Catholic periodicals.

GREGORY DIPIPPO, a native of Providence, Rhode Island, has studied Latin, Greek, Church Slavonic, classics, and patristics. He has been a regular contributor to the *New Liturgical Movement* website since 2009 and editor since 2013. His writings cover a wide variety of topics, but his first specialty was the study of the reforms of the Roman liturgy before the Second Vatican Council. DiPippo lived in Rome for almost thirty years. He is on the faculty of the Veterum Sapientia Institute.

MICHAEL BRENDAN DOUGHERTY, a senior writer at *National Review* and a visiting fellow for the social, cultural, and constitutional studies division at the American Enterprise Institute, is the author of *My Father Left Me Ireland: An American Son's Search for Home*.

ROSS DOUTHAT joined *The New York Times* as an Op-Ed columnist in April 2009. His column appears every Tuesday and Sunday, and he co-hosts the Times Op-Ed podcast, "The Argument." Previously, he was a senior editor at *The Atlantic* and a blogger on its website.

He is the author of *The Decadent Society* (2020), *To Change the Church: Pope Francis and the Future of Catholicism* (2018), and *Bad Religion: How We Became a Nation of Heretics* (2012).

TIMOTHY FLANDERS is the editor of *OnePeterFive*. He is the author of *City of God versus City of Man: The Battles of the Church from Antiquity to the Present* and *Introduction to the Holy Bible for Traditional Catholics*. In 2019 he founded *The Meaning of Catholic*, a lay apostolate dedicated to uniting Catholics against the enemies of Holy Church. He holds a degree in classical languages from Grand Valley State University and has done graduate work with the Catholic University of Ukraine.

MATTHEW HAZELL has a B.A. (Hons.) in biblical and applied theology from the University of Wales (Bangor) and an M.A. in biblical studies from the University of Sheffield. He writes variously on liturgy, the Second Vatican Council, and the twentieth-century liturgical reforms and contributes to the *New Liturgical Movement* website. He has published several important reference works, including the *Index Lectionum: A Comparative Table of Readings for the Ordinary and Extraordinary Forms of the Roman Rite*.

PETER KWASNIEWSKI (B.A. in Liberal Arts, Thomas Aquinas College; M.A. and Ph.D. in Philosophy, Catholic University of America) is a former professor of theology, philosophy, music, and art history, a composer of sacred choral music, and an author and speaker on topics concerning Catholic Tradition. He has written or edited over twenty books, including most recently *The Once and Future Roman Rite: Returning to the Traditional Latin Liturgy after Seventy Years of Exile* (TAN, 2022).

JEAN-PIERRE MAUGENDRE is the founder and executive director of the lay movement *Renaissance Catholique*, which works to promote the establishment of the Social Kingship of Christ. For thirty years, under the patronage of St. Joan of Arc, the association has been engaged in the pressing task of intellectual and moral reform.

About the Authors

JOHN PEPINO, PhD (Greek and Latin), is a Franco-British scholar interested in change and continuity in Church History. His work includes the translation from French into English of Yves Chiron, *Annibale Bugnini: Reformer of the Liturgy* (Angelico Press, 2018) and of *The Memoirs of Louis Bouyer: From Youth and Conversion to Vatican II, the Liturgical Reform, and After* (Angelico Press, 2015). He is professor of classical languages and patristics at Our Lady of Guadalupe Seminary in Denton, Nebraska.

REV. JOHN A. PERRICONE, PhD, is an adjunct professor of philosophy at Iona College in New Rochelle, New York. His articles have appeared in *St. John's Law Review, The Journal of Catholic Legal Studies, New Oxford Review, The Latin Mass,* and *Crisis Magazine,* among others. He is a popular retreat master.

ERIC SAMMONS is the Executive Director of Crisis Publications and the Editor-in-Chief of *Crisis Magazine.* He has published many articles online and is the author of several books, including *Deadly Indifference: How the Church Lost Her Mission and How We Can Reclaim It* and *Holiness for Everyone: The Practical Spirituality of St. Josemaria Escrivá.*

KARL GUSTEL WÄRNBERG studied philosophy and theology at the Newman Institute, a Jesuit College in Sweden, and sits on the editorial board of *The European Conservative.* He writes regularly for the *Catholic Herald.*

GEORGE WEIGEL, Distinguished Senior Fellow of the Ethics and Public Policy Center, is a Catholic theologian and one of America's leading public intellectuals. He holds EPPC's William E. Simon Chair in Catholic Studies.